DATE DUE

OC 7 '94			
NO 4 '94			
DE 22 '95			
MY 30 '96			
DE 13 '96			
NO 26 '97			
AP 7 '98 AP 22 '99			
MY 11 '98			
DE 4 '00			
NO 16 '00 DE 20 '00			
AP 5 '04			
DE 10 '07			

THE
EMOTIONAL
PROBLEMS
OF NORMAL
CHILDREN

Also available from Bantam Books

The Difficult Child
by Stanley Turecki, M.D., with Leslie Tonner

THE EMOTIONAL PROBLEMS OF NORMAL CHILDREN

How Parents Can
Understand and Help

STANLEY TURECKI, M.D.

WITH

SARAH WERNICK, PH.D.

BANTAM BOOKS
NEW YORK TORONTO LONDON SYDNEY AUCKLAND

THE EMOTIONAL PROBLEMS OF NORMAL CHILDREN
A Bantam Book/March 1994
All rights reserved.
Copyright © 1994 by Stanley Turecki and Sarah Wernick

Library of Congress Cataloging-in-Publication Data

Turecki, Stanley.
    The emotional problems of normal children : how parents can understand and help / Stanley Turecki with Sarah Wernick.
        p.   cm.
    Includes index.
    ISBN 0-553-07496-2
    1. Emotional problems of children.   2. Child rearing.
    I. Wernick, Sarah.   II. Title.
    BF723.E598T87   1994
    649'.64—dc20   93-23216
                                                              CIP

Published simultaneously in the United States and Canada

Bantam Books are published by Bantam Books, a division of Bantam Doubleday Dell Publishing Group, Inc. Its trademark, consisting of the words "Bantam Books" and the portrayal of a rooster, is Registered in U.S. Patent and Trademark Office and in other countries. Marca Registrada. Bantam Books, 1540 Broadway, New York, New York 10036.

PRINTED IN THE UNITED STATES OF AMERICA

(BVG)   0   9   8   7   6   5   4   3   2   1

To an incomparable woman—my wife
Suzie, with all my love and gratitude.

CONTENTS

PART II: A NEW WAY TO UNDERSTAND YOUR CHILD'S PROBLEMS

PART III: ADULT LEADERSHIP

ACKNOWLEDGMENTS

The families in my practice, and the parents and professionals who have asked questions and made comments at my lectures, are primarily responsible for the evolution in my thinking that led to the writing of this book.

Sarah Wernick, my collaborator, has brought formidable intelligence and writing skills, as well as outstanding professional dedication, to our venture. She quickly adapted her technique to reflect my personal style, and helped to expand, clarify, and organize my ideas. In addition, Sarah always displayed great sensitivity to the needs and concerns of parents.

Toni Burbank has been my editor at Bantam, both for this book and for *The Difficult Child.* Over the past ten years she has also become a close personal friend. Her deep understanding of the philosophy behind my approach and her support for some of my less conventional ideas have allowed me to write a book I'm very proud of.

I have continued to expand my horizons as a result of my contact with many knowledgeable colleagues. In particular I want to pay tribute to Stella Chess, M.D., and Alexander Thomas, M.D., pioneering researchers in the field of temperament, and T. Berry Brazelton, M.D., the eminent developmental pediatrician, author, and lecturer.

On a day-to-day basis, I am fortunate to be associated, at the Difficult Child Center, with Steven Friedfeld, C.S.W., a kind, gifted, and highly accomplished psychotherapist, and Wendy Padawer, Ph.D., a sensitive and talented cognitive-behavioral psychologist. Ruth Johnson, our multi-faceted office manager provides a warm and reassuring presence for parents, children, and staff.

I am very grateful to the colleagues, friends and parents who read early drafts of the book, and made many helpful comments. William Lockeretz, Ph.D., and Barbara Sofer—parents as well as writers and editors—applied their considerable talents to the entire manuscript. My appreciation to them and to Molly Anderson, Ph.D., Jonathan Cohen, Ph.D., Gail Glickman, Lisa Greenfield, Alfie Kohn, Lawrence Kutner, Ph.D., Marya Dantzer Rosenthal, and Tina Teken. Confidentiality prevents me from mentioning by name the parents in my practice who offered their ideas and comments, but they know how appreciative I am.

My heartfelt thanks to my wife Suzie, a caring mother and an enthusiastic participant in countless discussions and brainstorming sessions. She has illuminated many problems with her insights and suggestions. Even more important, she provides the love and support so necessary to my development as an author, psychiatrist, and human being.

INTRODUCTION

I am a child and family psychiatrist and the author of *The Difficult Child*, a book about young children whose temperament—the innate aspect of their personality—makes them hard to raise. I wrote it to relieve parents of unwarranted guilt, and to show them how to understand and manage their child's puzzling behavior.

My personal experience as a father and a stepfather has always influenced my professional views, so I am very open to learning from parents. Publication of *The Difficult Child* in 1985 greatly expanded my contact with mothers and fathers: I received thousands of letters and was invited to lecture all over the country. At these lectures I would often be asked questions regarding older children or those who were not particularly "difficult." Temperament in these instances was only one piece of the puzzle. Many parents were also concerned about problems that were significant enough to interfere with the child's well being, but not at the level that clearly required professional help.

Most of the parents at my lectures or in my practice had read *The Difficult Child*. Repeatedly, I heard that they had benefited primarily because my approach helped them to understand their child better and to look at his problems differently.

Gradually, as my perspective broadened, I began to think about expanding my focus on individuality and my faith in parents to a much wider range of ages, problems, and causes.

As I began to try out new material at workshops and lectures, it became apparent to me that specific suggestions for particular problems weren't what drew the strongest response from my audiences. Most simple solutions had already been tried by the parents. I found that I couldn't offer meaningful recommendations until I learned more about an individual situation.

Therefore, I started to ask questions about the severity and extent of the problems, the basic nature of the child, how the family communicated and parental attitudes to discipline. Often as parents thought about these issues and answered my questions, they would experience spontaneous insights and begin to look at their child and his or her problems differently.

Thus, *The Emotional Problems of Normal Children* does not aim to cover all possible problems, nor does it provide broad prescriptions to fit everyone. Instead, it follows closely the model of my lectures and my work with families, by providing a new perspective and the principles that will guide you to become an expert on your child and to devise solutions specific to your own situation.

Not only as a psychiatrist but as a father, I know how much parents hurt when their child has problems. And I have also seen many times the sense of relief and accomplishment that comes when parents take positive steps and see their child improve and thrive.

I wish you and your family every success as we begin.

Stanley Turecki, M.D.

PART I

NORMAL
CHILDREN
CAN HAVE
PROBLEMS

ONE

ARE YOU CONCERNED
ABOUT YOUR CHILD?

Ten-year-old Joshua looks miserable most of the time. He is easily disappointed and reduced to tears. Playmates have stopped calling, and Joshua says sadly that no one likes him. He has become whiny, and he shadows his mother around the apartment.

Joshua's parents, whose marriage has been in trouble for some time, argue about the best way to deal with him. Joshua's father believes that his son would make friends and feel better if he participated in sports. He has enrolled Joshua in a soccer league and insists that the boy join him for a daily workout.

Joshua's mother thinks her husband's approach is too simplistic. She urges her son to talk about his feelings. To boost his self-esteem, she compliments him lavishly and tells him often how much she loves him. But sometimes even she becomes exasperated by Joshua's behavior: She angrily tells him to stop pestering her and to go out and do something instead of just feeling sorry for himself. Afterward, she is overwhelmed by remorse and doubles her efforts to be caring and understanding.

■   ■   ■   ■

Joanna is four, and the director of her preschool has asked her parents to make another child-care arrangement by the end of the month. Joanna's teacher complains that she disrupts the class: She protests loudly when an activity is over and refuses to clean up; she won't lie down at nap time or sit still for a story. On the playground, she's too impatient to wait her turn for the riding toys and pushes other children out of line. The school director has suggested testing her for hyperactivity.

Joanna's parents are devastated by their daughter's expulsion from preschool. At the same time, they're exasperated with her, since she's defiant at home as well. Daily life—from getting Joanna dressed in the morning to putting her to bed at night—is a series of power struggles. Her mother feels humiliated and confused. She's bombarded by conflicting advice from friends, relatives, and even strangers who witness Joanna's public misbehavior. Her father, who occasionally explodes at his daughter's disobedience and swats her on the behind, guiltily wonders if his bad example is behind her aggressive behavior.

■   ■   ■   ■

Rosemary's mother doesn't recognize her twelve-year-old daughter. Rosemary, an only child, had always been loving and well-behaved. Now she's increasingly angry and defiant. In school, her usual A's have slid to B's and C's, and her provocative behavior recently prompted a call from the guidance counselor.

Five years ago, when Rosemary was seven, her father left the family "to find himself"; she has had little contact with him since. When her mom began dating again, Rosemary seemed enthusiastic. But her attitude changed when her mother became involved in a serious rela-

tionship. Last year her mother remarried, and things went from bad to worse.

Rosemary greets her mother's concerned overtures with a wall of impenetrable silence, punctuated by explosions: "Just leave me alone! All you care about is him!" Though Rosemary's stepfather tries to be understanding, the mother feels torn between her daughter and her new husband. The stepfather downplays the girl's behavior as normal adolescent rebellion. But her mother wonders if Rosemary has suffered emotional damage because she once again feels abandoned by a parent.

■   ■   ■   ■

Myra and Ellen, sisters ages six and nine, bicker constantly. They argue over whose turn it is to pick the TV show; who gets to eat the last cookie; who sits behind the driver in the car—and who is to blame for their quarreling. Though their parents bend over backward to be evenhanded, both youngsters seize upon their slightest inconsistency and accuse them of playing favorites.

The girls' mother, an only child who always longed for a sister, is baffled by the conflict between her daughters. Their father, whose own sisters became estranged as adults after a bitter quarrel, struggles to make peace between his girls. He lectures them about the importance of the family, and tries to referee their arguments. But no matter what he says or does, the fighting continues. The parents feel that sibling rivalry is tearing their family apart.

■   ■   ■   ■

Three months ago Tim's parents divorced, and he moved across the state with his mother and sister. Since then, Tim, who is seven, has been unable to sleep through the night. Sometimes he awakens crying from frightening nightmares. Or he comes into his mother's room with anxious questions: How would they know if a fire started in the middle of the night? Could burglars break into the house through the roof? Lately, he has insisted on touching each toy in his room exactly twice before he goes to bed. If he forgets so much as a single Matchbox car, he insists on starting over.

Tim's ten-year-old sister, who misses the friends she left behind when the family moved, resents all the attention he gets; she complains that nobody cares about her. Tim's mother is dealing with her own problems: She doesn't like being single, and she has trouble making ends meet because her ex-husband is behind on child support payments. She feels guilty about neglecting her daughter, but mostly she worries about Tim.

As a child and family psychiatrist, I see youngsters like these every day. They are not disturbed or mentally ill, and yet they have significant problems. I'm sure you can identify with their loving, concerned parents. We all want our children to be happy and to feel good about themselves. When they don't, we feel awful too. Underneath the frustration and worry there is often considerable guilt, and the lurking fear that something is seriously wrong.

THE PURPOSE OF THIS BOOK

This book is for mothers and fathers of children ages three to twelve, who are experiencing problems like the ones just described. If you're in this situation, you may have reached a point where you feel you've tried everything and don't know what to do next.

Discussions with your spouse and child may have become emotionally charged and unproductive. If your child seems unhappy, you may be tentative and overprotective; if the difficulty involves misbehavior, you may be criticizing and punishing too much. At the same time, you may dislike the parent you see yourself becoming.

I can assure you that you will see improvement once you've read this book and put its ideas into practice. But I want to emphasize at the outset that it isn't a "how to" encyclopedia, with specific solutions for particular problems.

Instead, I offer you a collaboration with me, modeled on the way I work with parents and illustrated by many dialogs and case histories. (Of course, all individuals are renamed and identifying details are changed to protect privacy.) We will approach this joint effort as co-experts. My contribution is my professional knowledge, objectivity, therapeutic involvement with many children and families, and a philosophy based upon respect for the individual. You bring your deep love, practical experience with your son or daughter, and powerful motivation to take action.

You will learn how to tap yourself as a resource for your child—no one knows her as well as you do. I won't tell you what she should be like; after all, she's a unique individual. But I will help you think about the person she is, so that your expectations are reasonable. Nor am I going to tell you how to run your family. My goal is to provide principles that you can apply to your own situation.

Underlying my approach are two basic assumptions that parents usually find very reassuring:

Normal children can have problems.

Expert parents can help them.

First, the fact that your child is having difficulties doesn't mean that he's disturbed or that there's something seriously wrong with him. Perhaps because of my personal background—I have lived in four countries and work in one of the most culturally diverse cities in the world—my view of normality is broad and encompasses a wide range of personal styles and preferences. Consequently I am very cautious about applying terms like "abnormal" or "disturbed" to youngsters with emotional problems.

Second, even if you are less than perfect and have problems of your own, you can do much to help your child. Expert parenting does not require detailed knowledge of child development; nor does it mean that you never make mistakes. Rather it is founded on a loving yet objective understanding of your son or daughter, and a sensible system of family discipline. You can't be your child's therapist, but you can offer meaningful support and make valuable therapeutic changes in his or her environment.

DOES YOUR CHILD NEED PROFESSIONAL HELP?

This book is not intended as a substitute for professional treatment. Though I emphasize what you can do, sometimes your own best efforts aren't enough. In that case, the book will help you clarify the situation and work as a coexpert with mental health professionals. Self-help and professional help are not mutually exclusive—on the contrary, they complement each other.

Emotional problems are a matter of degree. If a boy feels depressed, that could mean he's experiencing fleeting sadness—or misery powerful enough to precipitate a suicide attempt. A girl may express fear of the dark by insisting on a night light—or she may tremble and sob inconsolably. Knowing where your child's difficulties lie on a range of severity and complexity will tell you a great deal about the role you can play in resolving them. As problems move further out along the spectrum, it becomes increasingly likely that your best efforts will need to be supplemented by professional assistance. (See Chapter 12 for information on when to seek help.)

Let me illustrate the spectrum of problems and solutions by describing four nine-year-old boys who devote a great deal of time to playing with Legos:

THE NORMAL CHILD

The first boy is happy and does well in school, but his parents feel that he spends too much time playing with his Legos. He has constructed an elaborate space station populated with tiny Lego warriors, all of whom have names and detailed military responsibilities. If someone were to ask him if the warriors are real, he would respond, "What! Do you think I'm crazy?"

This is a highly imaginative, but normal child who requires no treatment. His parents should respect their son's preference, though they certainly could place some limit on Lego play and encourage his involvement in other activities.

THE NORMAL CHILD WITH PROBLEMS

The second boy became involved in intense Lego play after being hospitalized for epiglottitis, a frightening life-threatening infection in which the epiglottis—the fleshy flap that hangs over the back of the tongue—suddenly swells and obstructs breathing. His play has a medical theme and is openly hostile: Patients hit their doctors; ambulances run over people. The boy knows his Lego world is imaginary, but it comes to life in vivid nightmares. At school he's preoccupied, and his grades are slipping. His parents think he's dwelling too long on his hospital experience and have urged him to stop playing with the Lego set.

This is a normal child who is experiencing a temporary problem. Since he was well-adjusted before he was hospitalized, it's clear that he's reacting to a specific stressful experience. His parents can help by allowing him to express his feelings, instead of insisting that he forget his illness. They can ask his doctor to talk to him, to make sure he understands what happened and that he's now cured. They could also arrange for him to get extra assistance with his schoolwork until he catches up. These measures should help a great deal. But if there's still concern a few weeks later, consultation with a mental health professional might lead to a brief intervention.

THE TROUBLED CHILD

The third boy has been unhappy and withdrawn for more than a year; he has also been sullen and irritable at home and at school. Much of his free time is spent alone, playing with his Legos. He has set up a rural community with a farmhouse and animals. If he were asked if his Lego farm is real, he might reply, "No, but I wish it was."

This is a child with an unhappy family background, who has experienced other problems in the past. When he was three, his parents separated, only to reunite a year later. Two years ago his father lost his job, and the family split up again. The boy and his mother moved in with her parents, while the father joined a construction crew in another state. His parents' marriage suffered during their separation, and his mother began drinking.

Things are looking up now. The father recently obtained a local job, and the family moved to their own apartment. The mother has stopped drinking and the marriage is improving. The parents are very puzzled that their son continues to have difficulties despite all the positive changes at home.

This is a troubled child, whose symptoms are severe and chronic. His parents could talk to him about the past family problems, so that he understands what has happened and can express his feelings. They might arrange special father-son and all-family activities to rebuild relationships weakened by the earlier separation. Though these measures should help, they probably won't be sufficient: The boy's difficulties may have originated in outside stresses, but they now seem to be generated as much from within him as from the outside world. A therapist could help him resolve his unhappy feelings, and could also guide his parents.

THE DISTURBED CHILD

The fourth boy has always seemed detached and odd. Unlike the other three boys, he cannot tell that his Lego world is unreal. He refers to the Lego pieces as his army, and says he's a military commander from the planet Yklopki. He explains that he cannot go to school because his classmates are dangerous.

This is a disturbed child, the rare youngster who has trouble distinguishing fantasy from reality, and whose functioning is significantly impaired. He has a serious psychiatric disorder and will need long-term intervention to contain his symptoms. Such a diagnosis is a terrible blow to parents. A professional can help them mourn the normal son they thought they had, and the normal life they expected him to lead. However, they can be encouraged by their child's strengths: Though disturbed, he is bright and creative.

■   ■   ■   ■

Where does your child fit on the spectrum of problems? You may not know the answer now, but it will become clearer by the time you finish this book. In the meantime, there's usually no harm in trying new measures and waiting to decide about seeking professional evaluation or therapy. But I urge you to seek expert advice *right away* if your child exhibits any of the following symptoms: a sudden and very worrisome change in mood or behavior; bizarre or frightening behavior; conduct or statements that represent a serious threat to the child or to others. (See Chapter 12 for further information about emergencies.) Always err on the side of caution if you're uncertain.

TAKING A DEEPER LOOK

If you're worried about your child, you may have picked up this book and checked the table of contents, hoping to find a section that would tell you precisely what to do for his specific problem. However, this is not a book about minor child-rearing difficulties, so I can offer you no simple answers. If you're like the parents I see in my practice, you've already tried simple measures—and they haven't worked. This is a clear sign that the problems require a deeper look. What's needed is not a specific technique or solution, but **a fundamental change in attitude and approach that is based on greater understanding.**

When a youngster has persistent difficulties, parents often continue their habitual responses, even if they aren't effective. Over and over they repeat, "You're a terrific kid!"—but the child keeps saying, "I'm no good." Or they react to the same misbehavior in the same way, day after day, until the youngster begins to seem like a powerful adversary who can be subdued only by increasingly stern punishment.

As you read this book, three powerful realizations will help you move beyond ineffective responses:

- **REALIZATION 1: When simple solutions don't work, it's probably not a simple problem.**

Let me give you an example from a question-and-answer session at one of my lectures. A father stood up and asked me what to do about his son's lying. My initial answer stunned the audience:

> FATHER: *My son is a liar. We've talked to him endlessly about trust; we've promised that we'll go easy on him if he just tells us the truth. And we punish him severely if we catch him in a falsehood. But we still can't believe a word he says. How can we make him stop lying?*
>
> ST: *I don't know.*
>
> FATHER *(After a moment of startled silence): What are you saying—that it's hopeless? There's got to be something we can do.*
>
> ST: *Believe me, I wish I had a trick up my sleeve to make your boy stop lying. I'm not throwing up my hands and saying you can't help your child; I'm saying that I respect your efforts. The fact that you've tried so hard without solving the problem tells me that this isn't a simple situation. So I don't have any simple answers for you. But if you tell me more about your child and yourself, then perhaps I can make some recommendations.*

- **REALIZATION 2: If what you're doing isn't effective, the last thing needed is more of the same.**

The father quickly sketched the portrait of a suburban two-career family with three children, and he described two of many episodes in which his eight-year-old son had lied. I again surprised the audience by suggesting that the father stop lecturing his son about trust, and stop punishing him for lying.

> FATHER: *How is he ever going to learn to tell the truth if he doesn't understand why it's so important? And if we don't punish him, he'll just keep on lying!*
>
> ST: *Let me ask you something. Have your lectures made any difference so far?*
>
> FATHER: *Not that we've seen, but I keep hoping that our words will sink in.*

ST: *He certainly knows that he'll be punished if he lies—has that made him stop?*

FATHER: *Well, no. But he might lie even more if we didn't punish him.*

ST: *Perhaps, but I don't think so. If lectures and punishment aren't effective, the last thing you need is more of the same.*

- **REALIZATION 3: You, and not the child, must be the first to change.**

The father, like so many parents, was focused on getting his son to alter his behavior.

FATHER *(Incredulously):* *You mean we should just let him get away with it? I'm sorry, but unless he stops lying, I really don't see how we can stop punishing him.*

ST: *Part of the problem is that you're responding to your child instead of leading him. A pattern has been established: The more you punish him, the more he lies. And the more he lies, the more you punish and lecture. Right?*

FATHER: *That's for sure.*

ST: *You, as the parent, are the leader in your family. Therefore, you must make the first move to break the pattern. Before you can do this you'll need to step back and think very carefully about why your son might be lying.*

Finding solutions requires an understanding of the broader context. Lying could be a minor problem: Sometimes young children— especially if they're highly imaginative—skirt the boundary between reality and fantasy; if there are no other difficulties, their parents can treat fibs casually. At the other extreme would be deliberate lies associated with antisocial behavior, such as truancy or stealing from neighbors. This situation calls for professional help.

After the lecture, the father arranged for me to evaluate his son. I concluded that the boy lied because he couldn't measure up to what his parents expected from him. Lying was not his only problem; he also seemed sad and anxious. I worked with the parents to help them modify their expectations and adopt a more accepting and supportive attitude. Over the next few months, the boy's mood improved, and he stopped lying.

A NEW KIND OF PARENTAL LEADERSHIP

The ideal leader—whether we're talking about a parent, an executive, or an admiral—is one who can communicate effectively, and who is kind and understanding, but also firm and clearly in charge. Such leadership becomes possible once you shift your perspective. Rather than trying to "fix" the youngster or force her to obey, you will move over to her side. Instead of being adversaries, you will become allies, facing the problems together. This book offers four basic approaches to help you make such a shift.

PLANNED COMMUNICATION

The vast majority of parents make the mistake of trying to talk about problems when they're right in the heat of them. If that's true for you too, you've undoubtedly discovered that it's almost impossible to think clearly and talk constructively when you're close to a troubled situation and feel angry or upset.

I'll give you a communication tool that can transform explosive arguments into calm, collaborative discussions of family problems: **the planned discussion.** Parents tell me that this is the single most useful technique I offer them.

OBJECTIVE UNDERSTANDING

Negative feelings can easily develop when a youngster has problems. Much as you love your child, you may be disappointed in her, or even feel that you don't really like her. You may suspect that she deliberately tries to thwart you. If you've reached this point, I'm sure there is considerable sadness behind the anger. Feelings like these make it very hard to see the problems clearly and objectively.

I will guide you through an extensive **parental evaluation** that will help you examine your child's situation. As your understanding increases, and you begin to view the youngster more sympathetically, a burden will lift from your heart and the family atmosphere will improve.

ACTIVE ACCEPTANCE

Active acceptance is the choice you can make to accept your child for who he really is. This is not the same as gritting your teeth and settling for second best! Nor does it imply spoiling a youngster and setting no limits. Acceptance means that you gear expectations to your child's abilities, so that he doesn't disappoint you; it means that you recognize and appreciate his strengths. The more accepting you are, the more genuine pleasure you will take in your child—and the better he will feel about himself.

EFFECTIVE DISCIPLINE

Parents sometimes assume that firmness and discipline imply rigidity and punishment. Or they fear that structure and rules will somehow squelch the individuality of their child. But this isn't true. The firmness in my parental model refers to a system of discipline, founded on **strategic planning**, rather than on-the-spot reactions to the child's misbehavior. The idea is to set up a family structure—routines, clear rules and expectations—that guide him to success. The specific nature of that structure isn't nearly as important as the fact that it is carefully planned and clearly presented to the child in a calm way that solicits his collaboration. As I often tell parents, **the more structure and planning you can introduce, the less punishment will be needed.**

■　■　■　■

The fundamentals of adult leadership—planned communication, objective understanding, active acceptance, and effective discipline—are valuable at all times. But when a youngster is having problems, they become essential. As you begin to apply the ideas in this book to your own particular situation, you not only will help your child but also will gain a sense of yourself as a knowledgeable, competent, in-charge parent.

TWO

A PHILOSOPHY THAT
RESPECTS INDIVIDUALS

Few boys and girls pass through childhood without problems. The assumptions we make about these difficulties have profound consequences for the ways we deal with them. That's why I want to start by explaining the basic ideas that underlie my approach. Usually parents are greatly encouraged by them—I hope you will be too.

Some people speak of emotional difficulties as illnesses. This is done with the best of intentions: Using words like "disorder" or "disturbed" is a way of emphasizing that a troubled person should be helped rather than punished. But even though I'm a physician, I don't believe we should think of emotional and behavioral problems in medical terms. Using an illness model raises questions like: What's wrong with this youngster? What's wrong with his parents?

Instead, I start by looking at the total child—not just his problems, but also his usual behavior patterns, his strengths, and his talents. And because I don't think of children as mentally ill (except in extreme cases), I don't try to "cure" them. My goal in treatment is never to rid a youngster of every flaw. Rather, I try to help the child live more harmoniously with the significant people in his life—and, even more important, with himself.

My approach is guided by ten principles:

A TROUBLED CHILD IS NOT "SICK"

Emotional problems are fundamentally different from physical ones. If your child has a sore throat, and her physician suspects a strep infection, the diagnosis can be confirmed by a throat culture that looks for a particular germ. Once the cause is identified, the doctor can prescribe a specific medication that attacks the organism and produces a cure.

The situation is not at all the same with human feelings and behavior. Emotional problems rarely have a simple cause; the difficulties result from complex interactions among biological, psychological, and social factors. Though a psychiatric diagnosis may sound scientifically precise, it's based upon reported feelings and a clinician's subjective interpretations of what he or she observes.

Here's an example: Andy, age eight, is running into difficulties at home and school because of his high activity level, poor concentration, and impulsive behavior. This cluster of characteristics has been labeled and relabeled over the past fifty years, with terms like "hyperkinetic syndrome," "minimal cerebral dysfunction," and "hyperactivity."

Today's professionals generally follow the terminology and guidelines of the *Diagnostic and Statistical Manual of Mental Disorders* (*DSM*), which is published and periodically updated by the American Psychiatric Association. But in each of the three editions of *DSM* that have appeared since 1980 there have been significant changes in nomenclature and diagnostic criteria. The latest version, *DSM-IV* (1994), lists fifteen characteristics of inattention, hyperactivity, and impulsivity, and relates them to four different types of attention-deficit/hyperactivity disorder (ADHD). A child can receive a clinical diagnosis if he or she displays at least six signs of inattention or at least four signs of hyperactivity-impulsivity. These symptoms must be present in two or more situations (such as home and school) for at least six months and must cause significant distress or impairment in functioning.

That sounds very precise, but what does it really mean? All fifteen criteria are open to subjective interpretation—for instance: "Often fidgets with hands or feet or squirms in seat," "Is often easily distracted by extraneous stimuli," and "Often loses things necessary for tasks or activities." It's not hard to imagine that different observers would reach different conclusions about the same child, depending on what they regard as normal and what they consider "often" or "easily." Indeed, there is wide state-to-state variation in the diagnosis of hyperactivity, as indicated by the number of prescriptions of Ritalin, a drug commonly used to treat these children. In early studies, up to 20 percent of school-age children were classified as hyperactive—now current estimates put the incidence of ADHD at 3 percent.

After I met with Andy, his parents asked me anxiously if their son had ADHD. But this is not like determining if Andy does or does not have chicken pox. Here's what I told them:

I don't have a simple "Yes" or "No" answer for you. A child's activity level, impulsiveness, and distractibility can range from very low to extremely high. Andy certainly is at the higher end of the spectrum. But there's nothing magical about having six symptoms for six months. Suppose he's had five symptoms for five months: Would that really change the fact that he's having problems because he's very active and easily distracted, and that he could use some help?

I'm not suggesting that diagnostic terms and criteria be discarded. They're useful for research, for improved accuracy of observation, and as a shorthand for communication between professionals. I use them myself—though I interpret the criteria very strictly and require behavior to be extreme. But I'm deeply concerned that diagnostic labels are increasingly applied to normal individual variations in behavior and development. Over the past couple of decades, in sequential editions of the *Diagnostic and Statistical Manual*, the number of mental disorders has expanded considerably. Indeed, the present edition defines pathology so broadly that many of us could find ourselves within its pages.

Accompanying this change has been another that worries me: Because of pressures for achievement, especially among middle- and upper-middle-class families, having a truly average child no longer seems acceptable. Increasingly, teachers approach parents about minor problems and suggest testing; more and more children are labeled "learning disabled."

There's a real risk that medical labels—as opposed to simple descriptions in everyday language—can stigmatize a child and turn him into a "case." If that happens, it's all too easy to focus on symptoms and what's wrong with the child, instead of looking at him as a whole person. Treatments narrowly aimed at the "condition" can miss important dimensions of the youngster and his life.

Daunting medical terms may scare us away from commonsense solutions and into premature professional investigations and treatments. Parents sometimes arrive in my office with test results in folders two inches thick. These tests are often time-consuming, expensive, and emotionally draining; even worse, they can leave the parents confused and the child worried that there is something wrong with him. I'm *not* saying that professional help should be avoided—obviously, it can be enormously beneficial. Rather, we should realize that in many situations, simple, practical measures can be tried before going on to more complex interventions.

Seven-year-old Ned illustrates this point. He is behind the rest of his second-grade class in reading; he's often inattentive and occasionally disrupts lessons with angry outbursts. Because he's small for his age and not well-coordinated, he does badly at soccer and other team sports. His classmates tease him, and he's developed a nervous blink.

One option is for Ned to have a complete evaluation. This could include not only a thorough medical examination and routine blood tests, but also consultations with a neurologist, occupational therapist, educational psychologist, allergist, and child psychiatrist. Days of testing might yield such recommendations as tutoring with a specialist in learning disabilities, medication for hyperactivity, occupational therapy to correct poor coordination, dietary changes, or psychotherapy.

Ned's mom and dad are caring parents who would spare no effort to help their son. However, I think they would do better by approaching his problems another way first. The extensive evaluation could be put on hold. They could meet with his teacher and suggest that simple measures be tried first. Perhaps they could help Ned with homework if the teacher gave them a few guidelines; maybe the teacher could seat him in the first row of the classroom to reduce distractions and teasing. They could improve his self-confidence by encouraging activities in which he will be successful—piano lessons are a possibility since he's musically inclined. Having taken these and other similar steps, they could wait and see what happens. If the situation doesn't improve in a few months, professional evaluation and assistance would be appropriate.

NATURE IS JUST AS IMPORTANT AS NURTURE

A child's personality is formed by a combination of nature and nurture: inborn characteristics and environmental influences. Just how much each of these two factors contributes is a matter of controversy. While I believe that the adults in a child's life are very important, I'm among those who think that the role of nurture has been overemphasized. One unfortunate consequence has been a tendency to assume that if a child has problems, the parents are necessarily to blame.

I'm sure you've noticed similarities between the personalities of parents and children in your own and other families. While some of this represents learned behavior, it's increasingly clear that there's a genetic component as well. Studies of identical twins who have been brought up in different families find they're remarkably similar as adults, sharing not only physical attributes, but also personality characteristics and sometimes even emotional problems. Also innate, at least in part, is intelligence—and here I subscribe to the view that intelligence includes not only academic aptitude but also abilities in areas like music, art, athletics, and interpersonal relations.

My own thinking has been influenced by the research of Drs. Stella Chess and Alexander Thomas, who showed that temperament—the behavioral style of an individual—is innate. Chess and Thomas followed 133 subjects from infancy to adulthood. They discovered that nine temperamental characteristics—among them activity level, adaptability to change, regularity of sleep and appetite, and sensitivity to sensory stimuli like light, sound, and temperature—were evident in infancy and usually persisted as their subjects grew up.

This pioneering work has inspired further research on biological factors in personality. As you will see in Chapter 6, my list of temperamental characteristics is considerably expanded from the nine of Chess and Thomas, which were the basis for my first book, *The Difficult Child*.

If you have more than one child, or if you were raised with siblings, you already know that children from the same environment can be quite different. Here's what the father of Deirdre and Philip says about his daughter and son:

They come from the same parents and they've been raised in the same family, but they're like night and day. Sometimes we call Deirdre "Sarah Bernhardt" because she's so melodramatic. Last Saturday was typical. I said she couldn't watch TV until she cleaned up her room, and she put on quite a performance. She said, "I'll never be able to watch television again. The teacher will tell us to watch the news, and I'll have to say I'm not allowed. I'll fail social studies! I'll be a complete ignoramus!" She went on and on until I finally made her go to her room and close the door.

And then there's Philip. You tell Phil to clean his room, and maybe he'll sigh, but he does it. He's always been timid, particularly in new situations; it takes him a long time to warm up to people. We can't always tell if something is bothering him because even with us, he is reserved.

The differences between Deirdre and Philip were evident in infancy. He signaled hunger with whimpers, she with vigorous squalls. Deirdre startled at the gentlest touch, while Philip could sleep peacefully through a diaper change. She was always eager to explore and conquer new environments; he held back in unfamiliar settings. Deirdre displays her emotions with characteristic intensity if something is bothering her: She bursts into tears or explodes in anger, and may wake up screaming from nightmares. Philip's parents have learned to recognize his more subtle responses to stress: He becomes even more quiet and shy than usual; sometimes he develops headaches. Philip and Deirdre will grow and change, but the influence of external factors will continue to be filtered through their inborn characteristics.

The fact that many personality traits are partly innate does *not* mean problems are incurable, or that there's nothing you can do to help your child. Recognizing the interplay between internal and external forces will help you understand why different children respond differently to the same situation.

Here's an example: An outgoing girl from a military family thrives on frequent moves and enjoys having friends all over the country. But the same lifestyle is stressful for her two younger brothers, who are shy and less able to cope with change. Typically, one of the boys develops stomachaches in the weeks after a move, while the other becomes defiant and disagreeable.

Because their parents recognize the role of temperament, they give their sons as much extra support as possible before and after a move. They monitor the diet of the child whose distress emerges in stomachaches, and they're not unduly alarmed if he has his usual symptoms. The parents also are more patient than they might otherwise be with the unpleasant behavior of their other son, because they understand what's behind it.

DIFFERENT IS NOT THE SAME AS ABNORMAL

Your child doesn't have to be average! Most of us accept a wide range of behavior and personality in adult friends, but we're concerned if our child seems odd or different. I strongly believe that personal preferences and individual styles—even if unusual and forcefully expressed—should be respected and not confused with pathology.

Sometimes parents consult me because they're worried about atypical behavior. Tylene is nine; her parents are concerned because she has only one friend and prefers to play alone most of the time. I ask them how long this has been going on. If a youngster who is usually sociable suddenly withdraws, something is wrong. But Tylene's parents tell me that their daughter has always been somewhat solitary. I question them about her schoolwork. Associated difficulties, such as misbehavior or a drop in grades, would indicate a problem. However, Tylene is doing very well in school. Furthermore, she shows no signs of unhappiness or maladjustment at home. Taking these factors into account, I tell Tylene's parents not to worry so much; their daughter's behavior is unusual, perhaps, but it is normal and appropriate *for her.*

The parents of eight-year-old Eric bring a portfolio of his drawings when they consult me. The pictures are troubling: Eric favors bloodcurdling themes—sharks on the attack, soldiers fighting. I systematically question the parents and the boy. Eric is generally a happy youngster and seems to like himself; he has friends and does well in school. His relationships with his family are fine, though he says, "I don't like it when my mom and dad bug me about my pictures."

I tell his parents, "Your son has an unusual imagination, but he doesn't have a psychiatric disorder."

If your child is eccentric, but has friends and generally seems content with herself and her life, there's probably no cause for worry. At the same time, you can't completely ignore social expectations. If unusual traits put her in significant conflict with others, she will suffer from the friction. In general, I recommend that parents try to find or create an environment into which the child can fit comfortably. But when that's not possible, a balance must be struck between respect for the child's individuality and the emotional risks of nonconformity.

NEGATIVE BEHAVIOR MAY BE
AN EFFORT TO ADAPT

A child's "symptoms" may, in fact, be an unconscious attempt to compensate or adapt to a stressful situation. For instance, a shy and sensitive youngster who is withdrawing from contact with peers may be protecting herself from further hurt after a painful snub by her former best friend.

Of course, such efforts may be excessive and counterproductive. Nevertheless, it can be a relief for parents to recognize the positive aim of a child's negative behavior and to realize that the actions aren't irrational. Once parents understand what's happening, they can help the youngster find more effective ways to meet his needs.

This kind of awareness was useful with Ron, age six. Three days after he started day camp, his counselor called to express concern. Ron refused to participate in activities; he stood watching on the sidelines, sucking his thumb and looking unhappy. His parents were upset by this report, not only because their son sounded so miserable, but also because he had become whiny and clingy at home. They feared that behind his unhappiness and regression might be an emerging emotional problem, and they wondered if the camp was causing it.

I urged Ron's parents to look at his behavior from a different perspective. As they knew, their son was temperamentally shy and easily overwhelmed by anything new. There was nothing wrong with his day camp, but he had just joined a group of children he didn't know, in an unfamiliar place with new routines. Standing to the side and observing was his way of getting accustomed to his surroundings; sucking his thumb was an effort at self-soothing. His behavior at home simply represented a temporary regression to an earlier stage of development. There was no reason to fear something more serious at this point. I recommended that they give him extra support and understanding, rather than insisting that he move forward too quickly.

While most adaptive efforts of this kind disappear when they're no longer needed, they sometimes become ingrained. Deborah, age eight, carried tidiness to an extreme: Her stuffed animals were lined up by size, her bed was always perfectly made, and all her toys were placed in precise spots on labeled shelves. Friends were not allowed to play in her room because they would "mess it up."

Deborah's parents told me that her usual neatness became excessive about a year ago, around the time they temporarily separated after months of conflict. Though they had since reconciled, the behavior continued, to a point where they were worried about her alienating her friends.

I explained that neatness is their daughter's way of dealing with anxiety: She has made at least one part of her universe orderly and predictable. But why does she continue, now that her parents are together again? While Deborah's behavior could be termed compulsive, I find it more useful to look at it as an adaptive effort that has become a bad habit. I recommended that the parents tell her something like this: "We think it's great that you keep your room so neat, but it's gone too far." They would then limit the amount of time that Deborah could spend on cleaning and sorting activities.

PROBLEMS AREN'T ALWAYS DUE TO FAULTY PARENTING

A child with problems does *not* necessarily have problem parents. Nevertheless, parents—especially the mother—often are blamed when a child runs into difficulties. Parents in this situation may become very worried and self-critical. Their sense of responsibility, plus negative comments from others, can make them feel guilty and incompetent.

In virtually all instances, I can tell mothers and fathers that it's not only because of them that the child is having problems. However, it's also true that most parents could improve their behavior toward their child and help him more. Knowing it's not all their fault, but that they could do better, relieves parents greatly. They can then move forward in a way that's practical and constructive, without excessive self-criticism.

Youngsters experience difficulties for many reasons that have nothing to do with their families. For example, school may be a source of stress for a child—perhaps her teacher is unsympathetic, or she's being picked on by a classmate. She may have a chronic illness or allergy that affects her behavior.

It's also important to remember that parent-child relationships are very much a two-way street. While mothers and fathers certainly do affect the behavior of their children, youngsters are not merely passive recipients. Temperamentally difficult children have inborn personality traits that make them harder to raise. Such children, by virtue of who they are, shape their parents' style. Thus a person who is not normally tense could easily become an anxious, hovering father if he happens to have an impulsive son with poor self-control who is easily overstimulated and who often becomes aggressive.

Diane is a five-year-old whose temperamental characteristics— among them strong negative reactions to new situations, unpredictability, and high sensitivity to discomfort—lead to frequent misbehavior in public. Her parents get plenty of unsolicited advice from teachers, family friends, relatives, and even strangers. They were referred to me by a pediatrician after Diane threw a spectacular temper tantrum at her annual checkup.

Here's how her father described the episode: "My wife and I talked with Diane about the doctor visit ahead of time; we brought along her favorite stuffed animal. When she got upset, we tried our best to be comforting: My wife held her, but that didn't help. I took her on my lap and started to read a story. But she screamed and kicked, and we couldn't make her stop. I wound up hollering at her—it was so humiliating. Sometimes I think we must be terrible parents since we're raising such a horrible child."

Any father or mother would have had a hard time dealing with Diane at the doctor's office (and elsewhere). The preparation and soothing techniques that would have calmed most children simply didn't work. So if this beleaguered mom and dad look like problem parents, it's at least in part because they have a very difficult child.

I see parents as potentially powerful allies, capable of working with me on the youngster's behalf. In contrast to some therapeutic approaches, which exclude parents from the child-therapist relationship, I almost always recruit mothers and fathers as collaborators in whatever treatment I recommend.

PARENTS DON'T NEED A PH.D.
IN PSYCHOLOGY

Today's parents—and professionals—are inundated with information about every aspect of child care, normal development, schooling, and parenting. There are whole books written on subjects such as breastfeeding and toilet training. Mothers and fathers are told how to love their children, how to discipline them, how to stimulate them, how to make them happy, and how to avoid traumatizing them. Meanwhile, another set of books, aimed at adult survivors of various parental errors and abuses, offer a grim reminder of the price of failure.

Parents can benefit greatly from child-rearing advice. But they may get the impression that everything they do is highly significant for the child's future and that a single misstep could have dire consequences: If a mother has to discontinue breastfeeding because of an infection, she may worry that she won't bond properly with her infant and that their relationship will never be close. If parents can't find an intellectually stimulating nursery school, they may fear that their child will always lag behind his peers. This kind of anxiety is even more pronounced for first-time parents, especially if they don't have much chance to observe other people's children and to learn that youngsters can thrive under a wide variety of parenting styles.

Psychologically aware parents sometimes carry sensitivity to extremes. They may assume that issues significant to an adult have equal weight for a child. Or they may look too deeply for past causes when a girl or boy has relatively minor problems—especially if the youngster's history includes potentially troubling elements such as adoption or a traumatic event. This kind of exaggerated scrutiny produces what I call the **microscope effect:** Parents worry about the details of their performance, examine their children too closely, and get a distorted picture.

Here's an example: After Roger left for school one morning, his parents found his pet goldfish floating on top of the bowl. Roger was seven; this was his first experience with death, and his parents were determined to do the right thing. His mother spent her lunch hour at the library searching for guidance. In the afternoon, the parents talked about their son and his expired fish for nearly half an hour. They left work early and picked Roger up at his after-school program. Very gently, they broke the news, anxiously searching their son's face for signs of distress. At a local park, they held a ten-minute funeral, reverently burying the fish in a black pillbox. That night, Roger seemed upset and unusually irritable. This seemed to confirm that he was grieving for the fish, so they kept him home from school the next day and made an appointment with me.

The boy seemed tense during my routine initial questions, and I asked if he had any worries that he would like to discuss with me. He said, "I think my parents are mad at me or something—they're acting real weird, and they wouldn't let me go to school." I asked him if he was sad about the fish. "Nah," he said. "It's just a fish. My dad said I could get another one this weekend." I told Roger's parents they were right to consider the possibility that he might be upset when his fish died—but they didn't have to go as far as they did.

COMPATIBILITY IS CRUCIAL

In their research on temperament, Chess and Thomas identified the paramount importance of "goodness of fit" between a child's inborn characteristics and the expectations of important adults in his life. Children often have problems, I find, because of a mismatch between their innate nature and their environment. A loud, impulsive boy would fare poorly as the only child of finicky parents living in a small apartment—but the very same youngster could grow up happily as one of four siblings in a relaxed family with a large backyard. A girl whose shyness would present no problems in most families would run into difficulty if she were the daughter of a politician and was often called upon to be sociable with strangers.

A chronically poor fit does more than create external conflict—it erodes the child's self-acceptance. The youngster who constantly finds himself at odds with parents, teachers, or peers may begin to feel that he's a bad and unacceptable person because of who he is.

Mark, a delicately built and rather clumsy twelve-year-old, recently entered a junior high that emphasizes competitive sports. When teams are chosen in gym class, Mark is one of the last to be picked. He's been slow to make friends in the new school and is finding the courses a struggle. When he brought home his first report card—the worst he'd ever gotten—he told his parents, "I guess I'm a loser."

His father, who is a superb athlete, believes that competence in sports is very important for self-esteem and social success; he wants very much to help. He offers to work out with Mark and get him "shaped up." Mark enthusiastically agrees to a program that includes a daily early-morning jog and weekend sessions of one-on-one basketball. But he has difficulty keeping up with his father when they jog; after a few mornings he finds excuses to stay in bed. And he misfires the basketball so badly that his father wonders if he's doing it on purpose. Meanwhile, Mark appears to be even more unhappy and down on himself.

No one is to blame in such a situation: Mark simply lacks athletic ability; his father is a caring, conscientious parent who's trying too hard to help. Often parents feel thwarted when a child fails to meet their expectations; they may even suspect that the youngster is upsetting them deliberately.

The first step is to adjust their own thinking. In this case, Mark's father must accept that his son's talents don't lie in the sphere of athletics. Instead of continuing to focus on this area, the father could find an interest to share with Mark, such as computer games, in which the boy would shine. He might also try to make the fit better at school. Perhaps the gym teacher could be persuaded to include noncompetitive games so less-athletic youngsters could participate more fully. He could encourage Mark to join after-school activities where he would meet children who share his interests.

Compatibility works both ways: It's reasonable to expect children to adjust to their mothers and fathers, as well as the other way around. I am always aware of both possibilities in making suggestions to parents.

Any sensible intervention must be suitable for that particular family. If a youngster from a devoutly religious family, whose parents strongly believe in parochial education, is experiencing school problems, I wouldn't insist on his switching to a nearby liberal private school that would be more nurturing of his personality and talents, though that would be the obvious choice for a different family. Instead, I might urge his parents to seek a more sympathetic teacher at the boy's present school, or to locate an after-school arts program in which he could express himself.

Nor would I advise a high-achieving lawyer, whose four-year-old daughter was clinging and begging her to stay home, to give up her career. If the child seemed to need more maternal attention, I would help the mother find workable ways to meet both professional and parental responsibilities. For example, I might suggest that they wake up half an hour earlier each morning and share a relaxed breakfast.

A CHILD'S STRENGTHS CAN MAKE THE DIFFERENCE

A youngster's assets may be overlooked when difficulties demand attention. I believe that it's very important to nurture positive attributes, rather than concentrating only on curing flaws. Of course, you also should try to minimize the impact of weak areas—I sometimes describe this approach to parents as "making an end run around weaknesses." But the main goal should be to recruit and develop your child's strengths.

Eleven-year-old Leslie is chubby, and she worries about being un-popular with the appearance-conscious girls at school. Her parents believe that losing weight would help a great deal: A slimmer Leslie would have a better self-image and be more attractive to peers. They've taken her to diet doctors and enrolled her in an aerobic-exercise class. Despite their efforts to be helpful, Leslie has actually gained weight and seems more anxious and socially isolated than ever. Mealtimes have become very tense. Though her parents want to be supportive, they find it hard to remain silent when Leslie heaps her plate or takes seconds of dessert. Now they're wondering if her being overweight is really a symptom of a deeper emotional problem.

When I ask these well-meaning parents about Leslie's interests and special talents, they reluctantly mention that she's an excellent cook and very good with younger children. But these aren't areas they wish to foster: They fear that spending time in the kitchen will encourage overeating, and they regard her relationships with younger girls as an inferior substitute for friendships with other eleven-year-olds.

I point out that learning to cook low-calorie versions of her favorite foods could help Leslie to lose weight. Also, her success with young children not only will make her feel better about herself, but also will provide a much-needed break from the excessive focus on popularity in her peer group. Leslie might take a baby-sitting course: Among other benefits, it would bring her in contact with girls her own age who share her interest in younger children.

Sometimes an apparent liability can become a strength later on. The argumentative eight-year-old boy, who insists on negotiating every parental rule, may apply his debating skills to worthier aims when he becomes an adult. And who knows—perhaps the infuriatingly picky eater is destined to become a master chef.

One strength that all children share is a capacity for growth and change. Keeping this in mind—and remembering all the things that are right about your child—will infuse you with new optimism.

PARENTS DON'T HAVE TO BE PERFECT

Every parent, no matter how caring and conscientious, makes mistakes—I certainly have. As attentive as you are, you can't always know everything about your son or daughter. Children are constantly developing and changing, which means that uncertainty and error are inevitable parts of parenthood. Moreover, you don't have control over every aspect of your child's life. Bad things can happen despite your most conscientious efforts.

Your child also may be affected because family needs or limitations prevent you from doing what's best for him. Frank, who's shy and quiet, feels lost in his enormous junior high; he might thrive in a small private school, but his family simply cannot afford the tuition. Georgette's parents know that an out-of-town move is not the best thing for their daughter, who has many friends in their current community, but they've decided to relocate to a city with a first-rate rehabilitation center for the sake of her younger brother, who has cerebral palsy.

Children usually accept realistic limitations—provided parents are honest and supportive in presenting them. Honesty doesn't require extensive details. Frank's parents could explain that they can't afford private school—but they needn't show him the family budget. Georgette's parents shouldn't pretend the move is for her benefit. In both cases, parents can acknowledge that the situation is less than ideal and offer sympathy and encouragement to help their child make the best of it.

Sometimes—either because of poor judgment or bad luck—a parent makes a decision that turns out badly for a child. Here's one that was worse than most: Becky's mom, a single working parent, knew her neighbor wasn't the perfect afternoon babysitter for her eight-year-old daughter. But since she couldn't afford an after-school program and didn't want Becky staying all alone in an empty house, she brushed off the girl's vague complaints about the arrangement. Only months later did Becky tell her mother that the neighbor's teenage stepson was making embarrassing sexual comments and exposing himself; he had even fondled her a few times.

In my sessions with Becky's mother, she expressed considerable guilt. It certainly was understandable that she felt this way: She had made a serious error, and her daughter had suffered as a result; indeed, the child was seeing a therapist who specialized in sexual abuse. But Becky's mother needed to understand how unrealistic it was to expect that she could always protect her daughter. Continuing to berate herself wasn't going to help Becky.

Parents also worry about their personal imperfections. Sometimes when we aren't doing well ourselves, we assume we can't effectively help our children. Fortunately, this is not true. Obviously, the severe psychiatric disorder of a parent can affect a child. However, people with quite serious personal difficulties can be good parents—so long as they don't involve the youngster in their problems. I strongly believe that nearly all mothers and fathers can cooperate in sensible efforts to improve their child's situation.

Another common concern is that children raised in nontraditional families will be negatively affected. While I believe that a happy nuclear family is the best environment, I have repeatedly seen that children can be brought up successfully under many familial arrangements: by a single parent; by an unmarried couple; by a divorced mother and father who share custody; in a three-generation family; or living with a parent, stepparent, siblings, stepsiblings, and half-siblings. The caretaking responsibilities that were once the sole province of mothers may be shared or fulfilled by fathers, other relatives, day-care centers, or babysitters.

CHILDREN ARE RESILIENT

Sometimes when a child has significant problems, parents wonder if it's too late to help him. Even if they make positive changes and the youngster shows obvious improvement, they fear that trouble will resurface later on.

When parents express this concern, I can reassure them: A child's future is not irrevocably set by age three, or five—or even twelve. Nor does a single mistake, or an isolated traumatic event, necessarily become a permanent time bomb ticking in the youngster's psyche. Lasting harm is far more often the result of prolonged severe trauma, such as continuing physical or sexual abuse, or a persistently harsh, punitive way of dealing with the child. But parents (and some professionals) often underestimate youthful capacity for healing, especially with support from adults.

Another common mistake is to confuse a temporary, completely normal reaction to stress with a pathological response. The father of five-year-old Marissa was robbed at knife-point when he and his daughter were standing at a bus stop. For several weeks afterward, she was clingy and fearful. Her parents gave her a great deal of extra attention during this period: They relaxed their usual rule and let her use their bed when she couldn't fall asleep; if she brought up the "bad boy who stole Daddy's money," they encouraged her to talk about what happened and pointed out that such robberies were unusual. During the next few months, she occasionally had dreams about the incident. But after that, it was behind her. Marissa was affected by this experience—anyone would be—but she wasn't permanently scarred.

I find that most youngsters bounce back quickly when the cause of their distress is eliminated. If this doesn't happen, and the child's reaction to a stressful event seems prolonged and out of proportion—for example, a seven-year-old boy who still won't enter the school playground more than a year after breaking his arm in a fall from the jungle gym—professional consultation could be helpful.

Certainly parents should be aware of their child's life experiences and be responsive to signs of trouble. But a counterbalancing appreciation of youthful resilience is needed too. Children recover from adversity; they learn to compensate—and can even be strengthened by some types of hardships.

.   .   .   .

My belief in the fundamental importance of temperament and fit shapes my approach to children and families. I'm always keenly aware that a child is not simply clay to be molded by parents, teachers, or even psychiatrists, but a unique individual who is very much his own person. However, I view parents as the primary force for making positive change in a child's life. In the next chapter, you will see how the above principles work in practice, as I invite you into my office to observe the evaluation of an eight-year-old boy.

THREE

STEP INTO THE OFFICE OF
A CHILD PSYCHIATRIST

To help a youngster, I need to know about the problems he's having; but I also must learn about him as a person and about the family he lives in. I do this by conducting a comprehensive evaluation of the child and family.

In this chapter, I ask you to join me as I evaluate a child who was experiencing problems of a type I often see in my practice. You may recognize some of your own issues in this family, but the main focus will be on the evaluation process itself. I'll explain the reasons behind my questions, as well as my developing understanding of the difficulties. When you perform your own assessment in later chapters, you'll be following many of the same steps.

There's nothing mysterious about a psychiatric evaluation. In part, I'm simply organizing information and insights given to me by the parents—the real experts on their child. The evaluation usually takes about an hour and a half; it doesn't include an IQ or other formal psychological tests. My primary tools are observation and interview. From these I form a diagnostic impression of the situation and offer my recommendations.

My assessment of a youngster, and the suggestions I make concerning treatment, are based on three questions:

- **What type of problems does the child have?** Symptoms vary not only in their nature, but also in their severity and extent.
- **What kind of person is this child?** Problems occur within the context of an individual's usual personality—the traits and tendencies he or she displays when there are no special difficulties. I'm particularly interested in the child's innate nature, his strengths, and his emotional resilience.
- **What is the child's environment?** The most important environments are home and school. I need to look at both long-standing issues and recent changes that might have triggered the problems.

Sometimes, but not always, a cause can be determined from this investigation. If there's an obvious source of stress in the youngster's environment, parents may be able to correct it. But even if the origin of the problem remains unknown, the evaluation usually suggests ways in which parents could improve the situation. When symptoms are extensive, and their cause is unclear, it's more likely that the problems are rooted within the child. Such difficulties usually require professional treatment.

WHAT HAPPENS DURING AN EVALUATION

Parents reach me through a variety of routes. Often they're referred by the youngster's doctor or teacher; sometimes they themselves contact my office at the suggestion of a friend or relative. I also receive calls from parents who have read *The Difficult Child* or have heard me lecture, or have seen an article or television program about my work.

When parents schedule an evaluation, I ask them to fill out two questionnaires, one describing the child's temperamental characteristics, the other summarizing basic family information. (You will find similar questions in Chapters 6 and 7.) Answering these questions at home not only saves time during our meeting, it also helps parents organize their thinking.

Mothers and fathers often ask me what to tell their daughter or son about the upcoming visit. For a young child, I suggest saying that I'm a special kind of doctor who talks and plays with children and doesn't give needles—a reassurance the youngster is likely to welcome after hearing the word "doctor." An older girl or boy can be told that I help children and families with their problems. Most youngsters are relieved when they see the waiting room I share with my associates: About half the space is devoted to a play area with plenty of toys.

As I greet the family, I have my first chance to observe the child's interaction with his parents; often there are other youngsters in the waiting room, so I can also see how the child responds to them. We chat briefly, then I ask the parents to come into my office while the child remains in the play area under supervision.

I interview the parents first, questioning them about themselves as well as about their child. Then we go back into the waiting room, where once again I can see how the youngster relates to his parents and peers. Next, the child joins me for a private talk in my office; with a younger child who's reluctant to leave his parents, I may just play or talk with him in a corner of the waiting room.

When we're done, I remain alone at my desk for a few moments, organizing my thoughts. The remaining time is spent with the parents, sharing my observations and making recommendations. Sometimes, toward the end of this discussion, we invite the youngster to participate.

In addition to giving parents explicit recommendations, I try to make the evaluation itself a learning experience. I do not merely listen; if parents make statements that seem inaccurate or exaggerated, I question them and suggest other ways of thinking about the situation. My own interactions with the child model my suggestions. For instance, if I'm dealing with a distractible youngster, I establish eye contact before asking questions or giving directions. In this way the evaluation itself is therapeutic.

A CLOSE-UP OF ONE FAMILY

Eight-year-old Danny Cavanaugh and his family were referred to me by his pediatrician after his mother expressed concern about problems he was having in school and growing difficulties at home. The doctor thought Danny and his parents could use some help.

I learned more about the Cavanaughs from the forms they filled out. Matt Cavanaugh, Danny's father, instructs sales trainees for a major insurance company; his wife, Emily, is a librarian at a private junior college. They're in their late thirties and have been married for fourteen years. In addition to Danny, the Cavanaughs have a twelve-year-old daughter named Allison. Both children attend their local public schools; Danny is in second grade.

FIRST IMPRESSIONS

Though the door to my private office is closed, I hear the Cavanaughs arrive in my waiting room—first the child's loud voice, then an equally loud "Shhhh!" and reprimand from his father. I give them a few minutes before I go out to introduce myself.

The room is busy. Waiting to see my associates are a four-year-old boy, a teenager, and two sets of parents. The little boy is crying and clinging to his mother; his father is trying to distract him with some toy cars. Danny's family does not notice me right away. The Cavanaughs, an attractive, well-dressed couple, have their eyes on their son. He is energetic, with an appealing grin. As I watch, he rummages through a basket of puppets, frequently stopping to look worriedly at the crying boy. He spots the water cooler and leaves the puppets. The paper cup dispenser intrigues him. He pulls out three cups, one at a time, before his father interrupts him with "Hey! Stop that!"

His mother intervenes: She carefully explains that it's wasteful to take cups and just throw them away, and she goes into environmental details. Danny fills a cup and heads back to the puppets. On the way, he trips over one of the toy cars. Though he manages to catch his balance and doesn't fall, he spills the water. His father grabs the empty cup and throws it out. His mother finds a tissue in her purse and dabs at the spill. Danny's expression is sad. He returns to the puppets.

When they've settled down again, I greet them. The parents introduce themselves, but Danny ignores me.

MOTHER: *Danny, come over here and say "Hello" to Dr. Turecki. He's the nice doctor I told you about. Doesn't he have a nice waiting room?*

FATHER: *Now come and shake hands.*

DANNY: *(He looks at me over his shoulder.) Hi.*

MOTHER: *Danny, you know that it's good manners to shake hands when you meet someone. Please show Dr. Turecki how polite you are. (He ignores her; she looks flustered. I walk over to Danny, make eye contact, and introduce myself. He smiles at me.)*

ST: *Do you have toys like this at home?*

DANNY: *I have an Etch-a-Sketch and Lincoln Logs, but no puppets.*

ST: *Danny, I'm going to be talking with your parents first in the next-door room. Would you like to see where they're going to be?*

DANNY: *Nah, it's okay.*

These few minutes have confirmed some of the information I received from the temperament questionnaire: As his parents noted, Danny is loud, restless, and easily distracted. But he's also friendly and can separate easily from his mom and dad. I've noticed that his parents deal with him in quite different ways: His father seems abrupt, while his mother appears to rely a lot on explanations and reasoning. I wonder if this is simply a matter of their individual styles, or if their differences reflect other family issues.

INTERVIEW WITH THE PARENTS

The Cavanaughs come into my office and sit down in the two chairs across the desk from mine. They appear tense, which is to be expected. When parents ask me to see their son or daughter, I can usually assume they're worried about a youngster who is unhappy or behaving badly. The problem may have been simmering for a while, but probably it's reached a crisis point—the decision to seek advice from a child psychiatrist is a major one for any parent.

We have a lot of ground to cover. While I don't want to miss the subtleties of the Cavanaughs' concerns and observations, I must help them focus on specifics so the discussion doesn't ramble.

CURRENT PROBLEMS

I always begin by asking parents to tell me what troubles them most about their child. Later in the discussion, we'll cover any other problems; but first I ascertain the severity, duration, and extent of the most significant difficulties.

> ST: *Let's start by you telling me very briefly the main reason you're here today.*
>
> MOTHER: *I'm terribly worried about Danny, because he seems so angry and unhappy. He has temper tantrums and says he hates us. He's always down on himself; he has nightmares. Sometimes he says he doesn't want to go to school anymore.*
>
> ST: *Thank you. (I turn to Mr. Cavanaugh.) What about you?*
>
> FATHER: *Danny won't listen; he's fresh and stubborn as a mule. He's a troublemaker in school. The doctor said something about*

maybe testing him for hyperactivity if he doesn't straighten out soon.

ST: *I'd like to know more about the problems he's having at home. Can you give me some specific examples?*

MOTHER: *Yesterday was typical. When I came home from work, he was lying on the floor watching TV, and the living room was a mess. I asked him to put his things away, but he ignored me. So I explained how important it is for the family to help out now that I'm working. He just mumbled that he'd take care of it during a commercial. I was determined not to get into a fight, so I said okay.*

Dinner was a disaster. He picked at his plate, said he wasn't hungry—he's fussy about food, and I was serving fish, which isn't one of his favorites. Then as soon as I cleared the table, he wanted a huge portion of dessert. His eating habits are terrible. I was very patient: I told him how his body needs protein and vitamins. He said that ice cream has protein. We went back and forth, but finally he agreed to have a peanut butter sandwich before he ate dessert.

We finished dinner, went into the living room—and I discovered that he hadn't put his things away. I told him to do it immediately, and he yelled, "Oh, shut up!" At that point, I couldn't help myself; I blew up. I told him he was rude and lazy and selfish. He said, "I never do anything right." I thought I saw tears in his eyes. That made me feel rotten—to lose patience with him when he's already unhappy. I know he should have cleaned up, but I could've been more patient, and I didn't have to blow up. To make up for it, I let him watch an extra TV program.

ST: *Mr. Cavanaugh, do you have the same kind of trouble with Danny?*

FATHER: *Definitely not. I think he takes advantage of my wife because she gives in to him. Danny listens to me, because he knows I don't stand for his nonsense.*

MOTHER: *He obeys because he's scared of you. I don't think that's good either.*

FATHER: *Maybe I'm too strict with him, but that's the only way to get him to listen.*

MOTHER: *Then he gets upset and comes to me.*

The beginning and end of the day are particularly difficult. Mrs. Cavanaugh tells me that weekday mornings have been hectic ever since she returned to work. Recently, tension has increased because Danny has trouble waking up; he dawdles and complains that he doesn't want to go to school. Danny also has been putting off going to bed, saying that he's scared, and he often awakens with bad dreams in the middle of the night. His mother is concerned that he isn't getting enough sleep.

ST: *How long has he been having all these problems?*

MOTHER: *It's hard to tell. I remember he had a period of nightmares when he was three.*

ST: *We'll come back to his earlier history, but I'm talking about the problems he's having now.*

FATHER: *Well, he's never been easy, but things have gotten much worse since he started second grade—that was three months ago.*

ST: *Tell me about his problems in school.*

MOTHER: *We've had several calls from his teacher—they get into confrontations. She complains that he's uncooperative and fresh. Once, the assistant principal telephoned me because Danny was involved in a pushing match in the lunch line. He said that Danny often behaves wildly in the cafeteria.*

ST: *Has he ever done anything dangerous or mean?*

MOTHER: *Oh no—he's not a mean child.*

I'm not surprised to hear that Danny misbehaves in the school cafeteria. It's difficult for an active child to contain himself when he's been cooped up in a classroom, then moves to a far less structured and more stimulating environment.

The Cavanaughs tell me that Danny is in a large second-grade class with several rough children. The teacher, according to Mrs. Cavanaugh, is old-fashioned and strict. Clearly this is a less-than-ideal situation, not only for Danny, but also for his overburdened teacher.

> **MOTHER:** *She's frustrated with Danny; I can hear it in her voice. She wants us to do something about him.*
> **ST:** *What have you been doing?*
> **FATHER:** *We talk to him about his behavior all the time. We punish him—there's no TV for two days after a complaint from school. But he doesn't care.*

Putting together what I've learned from the temperament questionnaire, what I've seen in the waiting room, and what the Cavanaughs have just told me about Danny, I'm forming a picture of an impulsive, active, loud, strong-willed boy who is easily overstimulated and distracted. Such a youngster needs more structure than a lunchroom and large class usually provide.

When Danny's teacher complains to his parents, they feel responsible; yet they're also angry with their son and lecture him about his behavior in school. In this climate of blame and guilt, it's easy to overlook the possibility that the boy isn't acting that way on purpose. To help Danny's parents be more sympathetic, I must convince both of them, but especially his father, that his misbehavior in school isn't fully deliberate.

> **ST:** *Do you think he doesn't care, or that maybe he truly can't help himself? Isn't it possible that this big class, with all those other active boys, overstimulates him? If he's having problems in the lunchroom, maybe that's because he has a particularly hard time when there's a lot of noise and activity, and not as much supervision.*
> **FATHER:** *I never thought of that. I always figured he was doing it on purpose.*

I am pleased to see Mr. Cavanaugh's shift in attitude. When parents have a capacity for flexibility and change, solutions are much easier to find.

MOTHER: *Sometimes I wonder if he's resisting in the morning because he resents my working.*

ST: *When did you go back to work?*

MOTHER: *A year and a half ago.*

ST: *And yet this problem just started in September?*

MOTHER: *I see what you're getting at.*

ST: *You seem very close to Danny, but perhaps you're a little guilty about working and therefore are reading into him something he doesn't feel. The issue may be simply that he's not so happy about going to school because he's been having problems there. You've also said that things are very rushed in the morning at your house, and he doesn't deal well with that.*

I ask about Danny's relationships with other people, starting with his older sister, Allison. In the past, they've gotten along well, the Cavanaughs tell me. But recently Allison has complained that Danny pesters her and that his arguments spoil dinnertime and evenings. The fact that the difficulties are new suggests that sibling relations are suffering because Danny is under stress, and not because of some fundamental problem between brother and sister. Fortunately, Allison is busy with her own activities, which minimizes friction between them.

ST: *How does he get along with other children?*

MOTHER: *He's always saying he has no friends.*

ST: *What do you mean by "always"—how often does he say that?*

FATHER: *Not very often.*

ST: *How many times in the last four months?*

MOTHER: *At least three.*

ST: *Well, that's hardly "always." Does he get invited on play dates?*

MOTHER: *Yes, he does.*

FATHER: *He has his problems, but he's a popular boy.*

Mrs. Cavanaugh appears to be exaggerating Danny's troubles with peers. I wonder why she is so concerned, because his relationships seem satisfactory. Parents who are under stress with their child often magnify problems; distortions also may reflect the parents' personal issues. When I ask about Danny's self-image, Mrs. Cavanaugh again seems to overstate the difficulties:

> MOTHER: *His self-image is terrible.*
>
> ST: *Why do you say that?*
>
> MOTHER: *He must feel bad about himself with everything that's going on at school and at home.*
>
> ST: *You may be right, but that's an inference. I'd like to hear what Danny is doing or saying that makes you feel he doesn't like himself.*
>
> MOTHER: *For one thing, he says he's stupid.*
>
> ST: *How often has he said this?*
>
> MOTHER: *A couple of times.*
>
> ST: *Did he say this when he was upset?*
>
> MOTHER: *Yes—both times it was when I got angry at him for dawdling. I guess he wouldn't say something like that if we were just talking calmly.*

Mrs. Cavanaugh is beginning to realize that she's inflating this problem. There would be cause for worry if Danny had expressed a bad opinion of himself much more frequently, or when he wasn't upset. I'm also reassured by the Cavanaughs' answers to related questions. Danny doesn't show other common signs of negative self-image: showing off, bullying other children, or cheating at games.

I question the Cavanaughs about Danny's personal strengths and special talents. They tell me that he's kind and sensitive to other people's feelings; he also is imaginative and artistic, and can spend hours working on a detailed picture. Later I will point out to the Cavanaughs that some of Danny's problems mirror his strengths: Fearfulness is the dark side of his imagination; his annoying stubbornness is the negative counterpart of the same persistence he shows when he draws.

PERSONAL HISTORY

During the next part of the parent interview, I ask about Danny's medical and developmental history, as well as any previous emotional difficulties. I'm looking for factors that might increase his risk of having problems and any predisposition to develop certain symptoms under stress.

Danny's mother had a normal pregnancy and delivery. Danny was an active infant who had difficulty settling into a sleep schedule. Though he talked and walked early, his fine-motor coordination was delayed—for example, he didn't learn to tie his shoelaces until after he started kindergarten. Also, he wasn't bladder-trained at night until age four-and-a-half, a minor developmental delay.

Though Danny has always been "a handful," as his mother puts it, he's been through only one other period as rocky as the present one. I ask the Cavanaughs to describe that time.

MOTHER: *Let me see. He was three and had just started nursery school. After maybe two or three weeks, the teachers were complaining that he was disobedient and aggressive. That was when he had all those bad dreams.*

ST: *Do you have any idea what set this off?*

FATHER: *Well, things were tough for us. The month before he started nursery school, my wife had a complicated miscarriage and wound up having a hysterectomy. She was in the hospital for a week. We weren't sure how much Danny understood about all this.*

MOTHER: *When I got home, I was quite depressed for a while. I often wonder how this whole period affected Danny—whether it's still affecting him.*

ST: *When did he seem to improve?*

MOTHER: *It took a couple of months. By then he'd been switched to a smaller class at school, and I was feeling better myself.*

ST: *Danny might well have reacted to your sudden absence from home, and to your miscarriage and depression. However, being in a large nursery-school class also was a problem for him. But he's obviously a resilient child—look how quickly he bounced back. Has he had other school problems until now?*

MOTHER: *Not really. His kindergarten teacher told us he was socially immature, even though he was bright.*

FATHER: *Not his first-grade teacher.*

MOTHER: *That's right. She said he was doing well.*

Danny's developmental history suggests areas of vulnerability: His fine-motor coordination and bladder control were both delayed; his intellectual and social development were not quite in sync. I note with interest that during the previous stressful period at nursery school, he had the same types of problems he is having now—an example of the symptomatic consistency that children often display.

THE FAMILY

So far, my interview with the Cavanaughs has focused on Danny. Now I need to learn about the two of them and about their family life.

ST: *(to Mrs. Cavanaugh) Could you please give me a thumbnail sketch of the kind of person you are.*

MOTHER: *What do you mean?*

ST: *Well, I've already noticed that you really care about Danny's feelings, but have a tendency to exaggerate some of his difficulties and to worry about him. Is this just the way you are as his mother, or is this how you are generally?*

MOTHER: *I'm generally a worrier.*

FATHER: *Boy, is she! (He looks at his wife affectionately, and they both laugh.)*

I question Mrs. Cavanaugh about her childhood and her relationship with her parents. She tells me that she was timid and had trouble making friends. Her mother was a full-time homemaker and very supportive. This background may partly explain why Mrs. Cavanaugh feels guilty about working, and why she's so sensitive about Danny's peer relationships.

Mr. Cavanaugh also brings a personal element to his view of Danny. He comes from a large family, where discipline was emphasized. He describes himself as a "rowdy, hyper kid who easily could have gone the wrong way in life." What saved him, he tells me, were his strict parents and teachers. He's worried that Danny will get into increasingly serious trouble if they're too lenient. He believes that if he comes down hard on his son now, he will spare him much more serious difficulties later on.

By this point in any evaluation, I have a fairly good idea of how well the parents' marriage is going. Some couples broadcast mutual dislike: They sit turned away from each other; they interrupt and argue a lot, making sarcastic or critical comments. The Cavanaughs, I sense, have a good marriage; they confirm this when I ask them about it. Indeed, their main area of disagreement is how best to manage their son.

> ST: *You seem to have different views of Danny.*
>
> FATHER: *Yes. I think she protects him too much. He's much tougher than she thinks.*
>
> MOTHER: *You don't listen to him. And besides, you're not around enough to know him as well as I do.*
>
> FATHER: *I can't help that—you know how my job is. Even when I'm home, you don't listen to my opinions. We never sit down together to discuss Danny.*
>
> MOTHER: *Well, I'd have plenty of time to talk if you helped out more around the house.*
>
> FATHER: *Oh? Tell me when I would do that with my schedule.*
>
> ST: *You both seem to agree that more time is needed to talk. So it's really just a question of finding that time. You don't need hours and hours, provided you approach it in a systematic way. For example, you could accomplish a great deal if you scheduled a ten-minute discussion three times a week and stuck to an agreed-upon agenda.*

We discuss the main area of conflict between them: discipline.

MOTHER: *That's a major problem, because I believe in reasoning, but my husband believes in punishment.*

FATHER: *I think that parents should lay down the rules and punish the child if he violates them. I bet we wouldn't have all these problems if we didn't let him get away with murder.*

ST: *You both make valuable points: Mr. Cavanaugh, you have a good sense of the importance of rules and structure; Mrs. Cavanaugh, you're sensitive to Danny's emotional needs. But both of you have gone too far. You need to aim for the middle road, so you can blend these elements of firmness and understanding.*

Mrs. Cavanaugh describes several incidents in which she lost her temper when efforts at reasoning with Danny failed. Mr. Cavanaugh confesses to overreacting in a recent episode:

FATHER: *It happened a couple of weekends ago, before dinner. We had just come back from the playground after a good workout on the basketball court, and I told Danny to wash up. He gave me his usual argument—said he'd wash up later—and I said, "If I tell you to wash up now, you wash up now." Well, he went into the bathroom, but in a little while I realized that he hadn't come out. So I checked.*

There he was, up to his elbows in a sink full of soap bubbles, splatters all over the place. I managed to stay cool and just told him to clean up the mess. But then he gave me one of his fresh answers: "I don't have to clean up, because soap is already clean."

At that point I'd had it up to here with his back talk. I smacked him, and said, "Okay, wise guy, that does it: no bike!"

MOTHER: *We had promised him a bicycle for Christmas, and he wants it so much. Now I'm actually dreading Christmas, because I know how upset he'll be.*

FATHER: *Well, I feel awful too. I admit it—I overreacted. But there's no way I'm backing down. This kid has to learn who's boss.*

ST: *You know, it's okay for parents to change their minds. We all make mistakes, and correcting them is not the same thing as backing down.*

FATHER: *Well, I'll think about it, but it doesn't sound like the right thing to do.*

Mr. Cavanaugh feels guilty about his arbitrary stand. But he believes that any change of mind represents parental inconsistency and will undermine his authority. This belief makes it difficult for him to see the situation clearly.

FATHER: *The problem is, we're not consistent. If it weren't for my wife, I'd come down on him harder—the way my parents did when I misbehaved—and that would be the end of it.*

ST: *You're right about consistency—it is important. But I'm not convinced Danny needs more punishment. Look back on this week: Has he been more obedient since you told him he wasn't getting the bike?*

FATHER: *(He shakes his head.) Not that I've noticed. I guess I need to think about this.*

ST: *And Mrs. Cavanaugh, I gather that explaining and reasoning aren't terribly effective with Danny either. (She sighs and nods in agreement.) It's good that both of you realize your discipline methods aren't changing Danny's behavior in the direction you want. We'll be talking about more effective approaches later on.*

OTHER FACTORS

We've discussed Danny's family and school; now I want to know if there's anything else that might be contributing to his difficulties. I ask Danny's parents if any other people play an important part in their son's life. His maternal grandmother, who lives nearby, is very much in the picture. She has a good relationship with Danny, but unintentionally feeds into Mrs. Cavanaugh's guilt by expressing concern that he's suffering because she is employed.

The evaluation also includes questions about the family's ethnic or religious background; sometimes these are relevant to the problems or limit the range of acceptable solutions. Finally, I probe for any other pressures on the parents, such as money worries, drugs, or alcohol. It is quickly apparent that these factors are not significant for the Cavanaughs: Though they're in the usual time crunch of a two-career family, there are no other special concerns.

I end the interview by asking if there's anything of importance that we haven't covered. They consider, then shake their heads. I remind them that we will speak again after I talk with Danny. We go back into the waiting room.

INTERLUDE IN THE WAITING ROOM

The reception area is now much quieter. Danny is sitting at a table, next to a girl who is about his age; they're chatting and drawing pictures with colored markers. I'm pleased to see that he has calmed down and that he clearly has the ability to interact in a friendly fashion with another child.

Mrs. Cavanaugh greets him loudly and effusively, as if she hadn't seen him for days. "How *are* you? What are you *doing*?" she asks. When Danny shows her his picture, she exclaims over it: "Oh, what a *lovely* drawing! Matt, Dr. Turecki, come and look at this *wonderful* picture!"

Her approach is too loud, too stimulating for this easily excited youngster. He says, "I'll make another!" and begins hastily, without sitting down. The new drawing is much sloppier than the careful picture he made while his parents were in my office. Mrs. Cavanaugh will have to learn to be calmer with her son. I go up to him and speak very quietly, a pointed contrast.

ST: *Danny, it's your turn now.*
DANNY: *Let me finish this picture first.*

FATHER: *No! Dr. Turecki said he wants to speak with you now.*

ST: *It's okay—he can have a little time to switch gears.*

This too is intended as a model for the parents; Danny will do better with transitions when he is prepared for them. I watch him draw; though he's hurrying to finish, I can see he is indeed artistically talented. After a minute or so, I provide a gentle reminder by putting a hand on his shoulder. This time he doesn't object. He puts down the markers and follows me into my office.

INTERVIEW WITH THE CHILD

I observe Danny carefully as he enters my office; this is a new environment for him. He hesitates for just a second, then quickly goes in. This is not a child who shrinks back. He walks around, looks at the photographs of my family, and picks up the small clock that sits on my desk. I tell him that he can look at everything, but he may not touch; he puts the clock down very carefully. I give him another moment to explore, then ask him to sit next to me, behind my desk. Since he is a distractible child, I want him nearby.

During my interview with Danny, I will be watching his behavior, as well as listening to what he tells me. I want to find out how he perceives his problems, his family, school, and friends. I also will elicit information about his self-image and explore his fantasy life. Though I'm already fairly certain that Danny is a normal child with problems, and not troubled or disturbed, I will check for signs of serious psychiatric disorder.

ST: *Do you know what kind of doctor I am?*

DANNY: *My parents told me, but I forgot.*

ST: *I'm a special kind of doctor who talks with children and helps them. Do you have any problems or worries that you would like me to help you with?*

DANNY: *I'm worried that I won't get my bike for Christmas.*
That's what I want most in the whole world.
ST: *Is there anything else that worries you?*
DANNY: *My teacher gets mad at me a lot.*
ST: *Why do you think she gets mad at you?*
DANNY: *I don't know.*
ST: *I noticed in the waiting room that you wanted to finish what*
you were doing.
DANNY: *Yes. She gets mad at me when I want to finish what*
I'm doing, and she won't let me.

Danny tells me that a couple of classmates pick on him sometimes, but that he has lots of friends. He names four boys, one of whom he identifies as his best friend. Good peer relationships are a positive sign. I next explore his feelings about his family:

ST: *Let's talk about your mom. Is she mostly nice or mostly mean?*
DANNY: *She's been mean a lot lately.*
ST: *What does she do?*
DANNY: *She's always yelling at me.*
ST: *What about?*
DANNY: *If I don't pick up my toys, or if I'm not ready for school.*
Sometimes I don't know why she's yelling at me.
ST: *What about your dad?*
DANNY: *He gets mad at me too. He acts real scary when he's*
mad.
ST: *Are there any nice things about your parents?*
DANNY: *Oh sure! My mom makes these really good milkshakes*
with frozen yogurt and chocolate chip cookies. She tells me
stories. She likes my drawings. And me and my dad play
basketball and wrestle together, and it's lots of fun.

I'm relieved that Danny has good experiences within his family, but make a mental note to check that his father doesn't wrestle with him before bedtime; this is a child who would need plenty of time to calm down after a stimulating activity.

> ST: *I can see that you and your parents often get along well, but you don't like it when they get mad at you. Do you think you do things that make that happen?*
>
> DANNY: *I don't know.*
>
> ST: *Are you sure? I promise I'm not going to get angry at you— you can tell me the truth.*
>
> DANNY: *Okay. Sometimes I don't listen. That makes them mad. My mom yells, and my dad gives me a big lecture.*

This kind of acceptance of responsibility is unusual for an eight-year-old. Danny will be able to contribute when his parents and I discuss plans to improve his situation.

> ST: *What about you—do you get mad a lot?*
>
> DANNY: *Yeah. I get mad when my parents yell at me. If I'm playing basketball, I get mad if I miss a shot.*
>
> ST: *Do you stay mad a long time?*
>
> DANNY: *Nah, I forget about it.*

Here's a boy with a short fuse, but not one to brood or harbor resentments. I can reassure his parents about his anger.

Danny has become increasingly fidgety. Sometimes children behave badly because they've been asked to control themselves for too long. If they're given a break before that point, they're less likely to become disruptive. I tell Danny he can walk around for a minute. He jumps up gladly and goes into the waiting room. His mother greets him much less effusively this time, I note. They chat briefly, then Danny returns to my office and sits down again.

The next questions explore Danny's self-image. Though he feels bad because he's been getting into trouble, he's basically a happy youngster who likes himself. We move into the area of dreams and fantasies. This allows me to get to a deeper level of understanding. Also, I must exclude the possibility of more serious difficulties.

> ST: *Do you ever have bad dreams or scary thoughts?*
>
> DANNY: *Sometimes.*

ST: *About what?*

DANNY: *I have scary thoughts about monsters.*

ST: *Do you think monsters are real?*

DANNY: *They look real in the movies, but they're just pretend. Everybody knows that.*

ST: *What about bad dreams?*

DANNY: *Once I dreamed that I was a tiny red bird, and a really big tiger was chasing me. I was trying to run away. It was so scary. Then I remembered I could fly, so I flew away. And then I woke up.*

Danny's fantasies, like those of many youngsters under stress, reflect themes of aggression and escape. In an intense, imaginative child, who's clear about what is and what is not real, such fantasies carry no alarming implications. Responding to another question, Danny shows imagination and kindness, but also unhappiness and conflict:

ST: *Let's pretend I'm a magician and could grant any three wishes. What would you wish for?*

DANNY: *A bike! I want a bike so bad. That's my first wish. Then I want to be a superhero. I would start a whole group of superheroes that would go around and fight bad guys and help the homeless. I still have one more wish. (He thinks, and his expression becomes sad.) I wish I could always be good so that nobody would ever get mad at me.*

The interview is almost over. I ask Danny if he has any questions for me.

DANNY: *Do you have any children?*

ST: *Yes—you saw their picture when you came in.*

DANNY: *Do they ever get into trouble in school?*

ST: *Sometimes. All children get into trouble sometimes, and it isn't always their fault.*

   Danny, I think you're a terrific kid, and that most of the time when you behave badly you're not doing it on purpose. I'm going to help your parents to help you with your behavior. So now I need to talk with them. You can go back into the waiting room and play some more.

DANNY: *I think I'll draw another picture.*

ST: *I liked your first drawing very much. Sometimes children leave pictures here. Could you draw a picture that we can put up on our bulletin board?*

DANNY: *Sure!*

Danny beams when I praise him and ask for a drawing. I feel myself responding very warmly to this generous, friendly child.

We return to the waiting room. I stay just long enough to tell the Cavanaughs that I will see them shortly, then go back to my office alone.

PUTTING IT ALL TOGETHER

I take a few minutes to gather my thoughts into what psychiatrists call a case formulation. This is simply a concise, systematic summary of what I've learned, a brief outline of what I will tell the Cavanaughs. Here's my synopsis:

Danny is a normal eight-year-old boy with behavioral difficulties at home and at school. He has a slight self-image problem but hasn't internalized it to the point where he thinks of himself as a bad person. In other words, this is not a troubled child.

Overall, his temperament is mildly to moderately difficult: He's energetic, at times impulsive, quite distractible, restless, stubborn, and easily overstimulated. He is somewhat irregular in his eating and sleeping and has strong food preferences. These traits may be exaggerated as part of his current difficulties.

There is slight constitutional vulnerability, as evidenced by developmental unevenness and delays. His current problems have been precipitated by a change in second grade to a larger class with too many active children in it, and a poor fit with his teacher. There's inadequate structure at home, especially on weekday mornings. Discipline has become ineffective.

Danny's parents have a good marriage; their relationship is not a factor in their son's problems. They clearly like the person he is; however, his behavior does not meet their expectations. Issues in his mother's background cause her to exaggerate his difficulties and to be overinvolved. Danny's father is firm and structured, but his personal history leads him to be too harsh.

GIVING FEEDBACK TO THE PARENTS

During the final part of an evaluation, I present my thoughts and suggestions to the parents. I want the Cavanaughs to understand that they and their son have many strengths, but also problems that need to be addressed. When they're seated in my office, I begin with my conclusions:

ST: *I have very good news for you: I see no evidence of any severe problems or psychiatric disorder in Danny. He is having certain difficulties, as you know, but he's clearly a normal child. While there are ways that you could improve your management of him, basically you've done a good job with this boy.*

MOTHER: *I can't tell you how relieved I am!*

ST: *Your son doesn't always feel good about himself now—how could he with the trouble he's been getting into?—but these feelings are not fixed in his personality. Rather, he's showing what I call "wear and tear" from the conflicts he's having at home and in school. That's also the source of his fears and nightmares.*

FATHER: *This is all very good to hear.*

ST: *Let me tell you how I arrived at my conclusions. Danny is an action-oriented child, which sometimes makes him impulsive. He can become overwhelmed in a setting that's too noisy, busy, or loud. He doesn't switch gears easily and therefore needs help with transitions. He's very much his own person, with strong preferences that should be respected whenever possible. His current behavior is partly just an exaggeration of his nature: He's more* active, *more* impulsive, *more* strong-willed *than usual. That kind of intensification can happen when a child is under stress.*

Some of Danny's positive characteristics have their negative side. For example, he's persistent, which makes him goal-focused, but also stubborn at times. He's imaginative, which is terrific when he's drawing or making up stories. However, when he's under stress, he has frightening dreams.

Danny is obviously bright, but his development has been slightly uneven. As you know, his social maturity has lagged behind his intellectual development. While this doesn't really concern me, children who develop unevenly tend to regress a little more sharply than the average child when they go through a rough period.

MOTHER: *Should we be worried about his getting as angry as he does?*

ST: *No, I don't think so. He does have a short fuse, but think how much better that is than being a brooding child who internalizes everything. Also, I believe you will see an improvement as things change for him. I was very much struck by his openness and honesty in communicating with me.*

MOTHER: *Do you think he might be hyperactive? His pediatrician once suggested testing for that.*

ST: *Well, he's certainly a very active child, but I don't think he warrants a clinical diagnosis. Let's just see how he responds to the changes I'm going to suggest to you.*

FATHER: *I'm still worried that he's headed for trouble down the road. He's so disrespectful.*

ST: *Yes, he has run into conflicts with authority because of the kind of person he is, but with the positive changes we'll be making, I see no long-term implications for his character development. He's a caring, sensitive boy—I really liked him.*

FATHER: *You don't have to live with him!*

We all laugh; the Cavanaughs seem much more relaxed. Next I talk about the family:

> ST: *Danny is upset that you get so angry at him, but he speaks of you in positive and loving terms. I feel optimistic that I can work with you and help you be more consistent and supportive of each other in dealing with him.*
>
> *You have excellent qualities as parents; your marriage is strong; and you've shown me that you have the capacity to change. But the very characteristics that make you good for Danny in many respects have gone too far in some ways. Mrs. Cavanaugh, you obviously empathize a great deal with Danny, but you're too involved, and you look at him too closely. Mr. Cavanaugh, your focus on structure is very helpful, but you've become too harsh.*
>
> MOTHER: *So we're to blame for his problems?*
>
> ST: *Not at all. Certainly you could improve the way you're dealing with him, and I'll help you with that. But in no way is this a situation where you have harmed your child.*
>
> *Both of you are looking at your son through a kind of magnifying glass because of your own backgrounds. In your case, Mrs. Cavanaugh, memories of childhood problems with peers are causing you to exaggerate Danny's social difficulties. You compare yourself to your mother, which makes you feel guilty. You're also a worrier. All this makes you focus on his feelings with excessive concern.*
>
> MOTHER: *But I want him to know how much I care.*
>
> ST: *Believe me, your child is certain that you love him. Even if you were to pull back fifty percent, you would still be well within the range of what he needs.*
>
> *Mr. Cavanaugh, the behavior problems you overcame as a child make you regard Danny's misconduct with too much anxiety. A voice in the back of your head keeps saying that you have to save him from becoming a bad person, and that has made you too strict.*
>
> *Both of you have come to see Danny as an antagonist who*

> *has to be cajoled or punished into proper behavior. What we need to reestablish is an attitude of being on Danny's side—seeing him as a good person who is sometimes in over his head—and helping him through his difficulties.*
>
> **FATHER:** *I see what you mean about a different attitude, but I'm not sure how that will get him to behave himself at school.*

I explain that Danny doesn't misbehave on purpose: To a great extent, his difficulties at school reflect the overstimulating environment and a poor fit with his teacher. I point out that highly active children thrive on structure and predictability. I recommend that the Cavanaughs request a conference with Danny's teacher.

> **ST:** *You have a lot of useful information to offer. It also would be helpful if you let the teacher know you understand she's frustrated with him and with her large and difficult class. You might suggest a few simple ideas—for example, that she seat Danny near the front of the room and establish eye contact before she gives him instructions. If you sense that she's willing to do more, propose that she arrange a brief calm-down period for Danny after lunch, before he returns to class. If she does this, she should explain to him that it's not a punishment, but a way to help him get ready for the afternoon.*
>
> **MOTHER:** *Those are good ideas. I just hope she's willing to go along with them.*
>
> **ST:** *If you wish, you can tell her you've seen me. I'd be glad to talk with her.*
>
> **MOTHER:** *Thanks—I'll mention that at our conference.*
>
> **ST:** *In the meantime, I think you should tell Danny that a lot of the times he gets into trouble at school are not his fault. So from now on, he's not going to be punished at home for anything that he does at school.*
>
> **FATHER:** *Wait a minute! That's giving him license to misbehave!*
>
> **ST:** *Not at all. Explain that you think things will get better and that you want him to try harder. I believe this will have a positive effect on Danny.*

> MOTHER: *It would be a great relief not to punish him so much.*

I point out that they've been *responding* to misbehavior, rather than *planning* to prevent it. This pattern has created a vicious circle, in which their repeated reasoning, yelling, and punishing only reinforce Danny's rudeness and defiance.

> ST: *You need more consistency and structure, and less reasoning and punishment.*
>
> MOTHER: *I'm not sure I understand why it's wrong to reason with a child.*
>
> ST: *It's not wrong, but there's no point giving the same explanation over and over again, or getting into a lengthy negotiation when you know perfectly well that you aren't going to change your mind. In these cases, you can avoid frustrating interactions by taking a stand early and bringing the discussion to an end.*
>
> FATHER: *What about punishment?*
>
> ST: *That's a very small component of discipline. The more structure and predictability you have, and the more you deal with your child in a kind and firm way, the less you will have to punish.*
>
> FATHER: *That would be a nice change—if it works. I must say, I like the idea of being kind to him.*
>
> ST: *You also need to pull back in certain areas. I sometimes suggest that parents make up lists of all the bothersome behaviors, then get together and decide on priorities. Let go of the little things, and save your energy for what's truly important.*
>
> FATHER: *My wife worries too much about what he eats.*
>
> MOTHER: *Well, I happen to believe that good nutrition is important.*
>
> FATHER: *You're right, but it wouldn't kill him if he had a sandwich or cold cereal for supper when he doesn't like what we're eating.*
>
> MOTHER: *I guess that would be okay. It's awful when dinner is ruined by an argument.*

> ST: *There's an excellent example of pulling back. His preferences should be respected as much as possible.*
>
> *You need to plan more friendly activities for Danny to share with his father. He told me that he enjoys wrestling and playing basketball with you, Mr. Cavanaugh.*
>
> FATHER: *My neighbor and his son are on a father-son basketball team—we'd both enjoy that. I'll look into it tomorrow.*
>
> ST: *Good. I also made a note to suggest that you avoid roughhousing with Danny before bedtime, since it would get him too revved up.*
>
> *And another note about your evenings: Better planning would make mornings less rushed for your family. For example, you might be able to take care of some tasks the night before.*
>
> MOTHER: *I guess we could get the table set for breakfast and make sure Danny's clothes are ready for the next day. I do that when I have time, which isn't very often.*
>
> FATHER: *I could handle the dishes.*
>
> MOTHER: *That would help.*

I explain that it's important to tell Danny ahead of time about new rules and other changes at home. At this point Mrs. Cavanaugh stops me, saying she would like to take notes; we review some of the major points. I suggest, and the Cavanaughs agree, that we meet a few times without Danny and that I check him after those meetings to see how he's doing.

> ST: *Let's tell Danny some of the things we've decided.*
>
> FATHER: *I'll get him. (He opens the door to the waiting room and beckons to Danny. He gives the boy a warm hug and brings him into the office. Danny sits next to me.)*
>
> ST: *Danny, I've told your parents that I think you're a great kid and that you have a very nice family. There have been some problems, but Dad and Mom are going to take care of those now. Your family will have some new rules to help you all get along better. I want you to do your very best to cooperate with them.*
>
> MOTHER: *And we're getting rid of some old rules.*
>
> DANNY: *Like what?*

> **FATHER:** *Mom and I decided that you don't have to eat foods that you don't like. So when we're having fish for dinner, you can have cold cereal or a sandwich.*
>
> **DANNY:** *Cheerios for dinner—that's great! What about oatmeal cookies for breakfast?*
>
> **MOTHER:** *Cookies have too much sugar and— (She starts to explain, then catches herself.) No. Cookies aren't breakfast food in our house.*
>
> **ST:** *Good! Danny, I'll see your parents a few times, then you'll come and tell me how you are doing.*
>
> **DANNY:** *Okay.*

I accompany Danny and his parents to the waiting room. Danny gives me the drawing he's been working on, and I hang it on my bulletin board while the Cavanaughs watch.

THE FOLLOW-UP VISIT

I had three sessions with Mr. and Mrs. Cavanaugh, and a fourth in which I spoke with Danny as well as his parents. My chief aims were to strengthen discipline and promote positive interactions between Danny and his parents.

At our first meeting, we devised routines to make mornings and evenings less harried. Mrs. Cavanaugh decided to wake up fifteen minutes earlier to reduce the pressure she was feeling. Certain preparations—setting out clothing, assembling homework, putting breakfast dishes on the kitchen table—became part of the evening routine. Though the new system, which applied only to weekdays, broke down the first few Sunday evenings and Monday mornings, the Cavanaughs saw an immediate improvement.

Both parents changed their approach to Danny. Mrs. Cavanaugh became firmer, though she continued, out of habit, to overexplain at times. However, once Danny realized that an explained "No" didn't mean "Maybe," he became less interested in prolonged negotiations.

Mr. Cavanaugh, who had always been a loving and involved father despite his strictness, took steps to strengthen his relationship with Danny. In addition to their own basketball sessions, they joined an informal father-son group that played on Saturday afternoons. Mr. Cavanaugh also began reading to his son every night. The second time I met with the Cavanaughs alone, I was particularly happy to hear that he had changed his mind: Danny would get a bicycle for Christmas after all.

As I had expected, Danny made useful contributions to planning changes. He realized on his own that most of his problems in the school cafeteria occurred when he stood in line with a certain classmate who often teased him. He decided to wait a few minutes and stand with his best friend, who attended a pull-out program and arrived after the rest of the class.

Danny's teacher initially was skeptical about the Cavanaughs' suggestions but, to her credit, was willing to try. Though she didn't make all the changes we would have liked—in part because she was overburdened by her class—the friction between her and Danny eased considerably.

By the time Danny and his parents came for his follow-up visit, two months after the evaluation, the situation had greatly improved. During the past month, there had been no complaints from school. The Cavanaughs described their son as noticeably more cheerful and cooperative; these days he hardly ever had bad dreams. They were delighted not only with the changes in him, but with the generally improved atmosphere in their family.

I asked Danny how things were going. "Me and my dad are on this basketball team, and he's going to take me to a Knicks game," he told me. "Everything's cool."

∎   ∎   ∎   ∎

As I explained at the outset—and as you can see from Danny's evaluation—a considerable part of my role is to elicit and organize information that parents already have about their child. Part II of this book, which shows you how to examine your situation systematically and objectively, will enable you to do this for yourself.

PART II

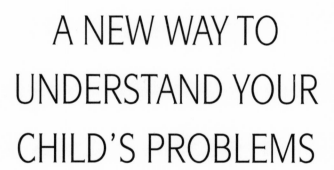

A NEW WAY TO UNDERSTAND YOUR CHILD'S PROBLEMS

FOUR

PLANNED COMMUNICATION

Family communication is never more important—and never more difficult—than when a child has problems. Heated emotions are only natural at such a time. Conversations can quickly turn into arguments; you may find yourself saying the same things over and over. At the end, nothing has been achieved, and you're left with a sense of going round in circles. This chapter will show you how to recognize these patterns—and move beyond them.

How can you think clearly and speak calmly when your feelings are overwhelming? Not by suppressing your emotions or weighing every word you utter—that's not realistic. And there's little hope of giving a troubling situation thoughtful attention if you haven't dealt with the reactions it stirs. However, the expression of feeling and objective thinking cannot occur simultaneously. Each must get its due—but separately.

This chapter presents a powerful technique for achieving a problem-solving attitude: **the planned discussion.** This is a serious and deliberate talk, which takes place when everyone is calm and focused on the subject at hand.

My concern here is not with facilitating family openness in general, important as that is. The focus is on using communication as a tool to evaluate and address your child's problems. This will prepare you for the parental evaluation that follows in Chapters 5, 6, and 7. And as you will see in Part III, the same principles will help your family collaborate on solutions.

WHY COMMUNICATION GOES ASTRAY

If you're deeply concerned about your child, but can't seem to talk effectively about the problems with her or with your spouse, the experience of the family described below will sound familiar. As you read it, see if you can figure out why things went wrong:

Kirsten's parents have met at a supermarket after work. Their daughter is eleven, and she's been getting into trouble in school. As they fill a grocery cart, the mother describes the latest episode.

"I got another call from the principal today," she says grimly. "Kirsten really did it this time. She swore at her teacher, which was bad enough. Then, when the teacher told her to go to the office, she said, 'Make me.' The principal and a gym teacher had to drag her out. She's suspended for the rest of the week, and we have to come in with her for a conference first thing Monday morning."

The father is horrified. "My God, that's terrible!" he says. "I'm very worried—this isn't like Kirsten." They reach the produce counter and stop talking to make their selections.

"You know, she's exactly the same way at home," says the mother as they move on. "You don't seem to realize how uncooperative and fresh she is—maybe not to you, but certainly to me."

"Oh, she's not so bad for a preadolescent."

"Daddy's precious little girl can do no wrong," the mother says sarcastically. "What about swearing at the teacher? Do you call that 'Not so bad'?"

"No, of course that's important," he says. "We've got to talk to her about it." They realize that it's getting late and stop talking to focus on shopping. Ten minutes later, they're on the checkout line.

The mother says, "Well, I told you last time we should have grounded her with no TV. Then she would have thought twice before opening her big mouth today."

"I want to hear her side of this before I jump to conclusions," the father says. They reach the cashier and start unloading their groceries from the cart.

When they arrive home, Kirsten greets them with a disagreeable, "Oh. It's you."

"The principal called me today, Kirsten," responds her mother curtly. "Your father and I will talk to you after dinner."

"Oh, who cares," mutters Kirsten. She goes to her room and slams the door. Later, when her mother calls her for dinner, Kirsten yells back, "I'm not hungry. Besides, the food around here sucks!"

The mother looks at her husband. "See?" she says bitterly.

As the parents finish a quick, tense dinner, the telephone rings. The mother answers; the father goes to his desk.

When the mother finishes her call, she goes to the family room. Kirsten is watching television, and her husband is at his desk paying bills. "We have to talk," she says.

"When the show is over," says Kirsten, not moving her eyes from the TV.

"No, now!" insists the mother. Kirsten ignores her.

"Just give me three minutes," says the father. He continues to scribble. The mother is annoyed. "You're as bad as she is!" She turns off the TV. Kirsten tries to reach the switch, but her mother pushes her hand away.

"You could have waited a few minutes," says the father. But he stops working and turns his chair to face his wife; she remains standing. Kirsten slumps on the sofa, her arms folded across her chest and her face sullen.

The mother begins: "What's going on at school? There's no excuse for what happened today!"

"The teacher is mean, and—" Kirsten begins.

The father interrupts: "I doubt that the teacher is really mean; she's just strict. I had a very strict teacher in sixth grade, and at first I thought she *was mean. But she taught us a lot, and gradually I started to appreciate her. Kirsten, I'm sure you'd like your teacher if you gave her a chance."*

"No I wouldn't!" shouts Kirsten. "I hate her! She's always picking on me."

"I find that very hard to believe," says her mother. "Knowing you, I bet you're doing something to make her angry."

Kirsten explodes: "You always take her side. You don't care about me! The teacher is a bitch, and so are you!" She storms out of the room.

Her mother yells after her, "One more call from school and you're grounded for the month. And no more TV tonight for being so fresh!"

"Very good," says the father sarcastically. "That really helps."

"Why don't you try dealing with her for a change, instead of just criticizing me?" she retorts.

The father returns to his checkbook without answering. The mother switches on the TV. There's no point continuing: They're both exhausted, and besides, they've had this argument before.

Kirsten's parents are worried about their daughter, and they want to do something. But so far, talking hasn't helped. Here's why they run into trouble:

- *Too many distractions.* Kirsten's difficulties are competing for attention with grocery shopping, the telephone, the TV, and the checkbook.
- *Adversarial positions.* Family members see themselves as opponents. They take sides; they accuse each other.
- *Intrusive emotions.* The mother is angry at her daughter and at her husband; both parents are upset and worried about Kirsten. She, in turn, is furious with her mother. Their discussions are dominated by these feelings.
- *Sore points.* Unresolved issues and old arguments have resurfaced. Statements and behavior acquire added significance, causing exaggerated reactions.
- *Lack of focus.* Conversations are a hodgepodge of questions and assertions. They yield no additional information.

- *Premature efforts at solutions.* Kirsten's father tries to change his daughter's mind about her teacher, though she's in no mood to listen; the mother threatens to punish her. The parents are attempting to solve the problem without first finding out what has happened and figuring out why.

RECOGNIZING YOUR HIDDEN EMOTIONS

If you're struggling with confusing problems, your feelings may be unclear as well. When a youngster is in trouble, parents respond on many levels. They may complain a lot and voice anger or frustration with the child; they may be defensive and blame each other, while denying their own responsibility. Such reactions disguise deeper emotions, such as guilt, worry, sadness, and a sense of impotence.

These hidden emotions often become visible in my work with families of temperamentally difficult children. Eddie's parents are an example. Their son was a very difficult six-year-old—demanding, stubborn, very active, and impulsive. Because Eddie's mom became angry at him so frequently, his dad had instinctively slipped into the role of Eddie's defender. When I asked her for an example of his behavior, she described an incident in which he pulled out a refrigerator shelf, sending eggs and glass containers crashing to the floor.

"So I'm down on my hands and knees cleaning up the mess, yelling at Eddie for disobeying, and in walks his father," she said, clearly upset at the memory. "Instead of helping me, he starts with, 'Look, kids have accidents. He didn't do it on purpose.'"

Her husband interrupted: "Well, he didn't."

Eddie's mother flushed, and she seemed ready to make a hostile retort. I already knew that she was a full-time homemaker, that the boy had two younger brothers, and that the family lived in a crowded apartment. So I commented sympathetically, "Things must be terribly difficult for you." To her husband's astonishment, she began to cry.

I explained her tears to him: "You've only seen your wife's anger, but underneath her complaints about Eddie is the message, 'I'm not coping; I need your support.' " He understood immediately, and put his arms around her.

Expressing your feelings, and having them acknowledged by your spouse, is tremendously helpful. But articulating needs can be difficult. We sometimes expect our partners to read our minds or intuitively understand our feelings, and to come forward without being asked. Not surprisingly, this often leads to disappointment.

We may resist acknowledging that we are in over our heads, especially if this means we must request help from someone who has angered us. Or we may feel ashamed of our emotions. As a result, our needs are expressed in a distorted or exaggerated way. For instance, they may emerge in an angry outburst, which pushes other people away when we really want them to be closer and more available.

There's no simple solution, no magic formula to make it easy to express your deepest feelings. But if you can manage to explain your needs frankly and directly, your spouse is much more likely to respond positively.

EXPRESSING FEELINGS VERSUS VENTING THEM

When you're angry or upset, how do you let your spouse and child know how you feel, without saying something you'll later regret? I find it useful to distinguish between a straightforward expression of feelings, and a more explosive ventilation of emotions. Venting reactions are often out of proportion and reflect not only the present situation but also past experiences or inner turmoil.

Here's an illustration: A mother asks her twelve-year-old daughter to help her clean up after dinner, and the girl refuses. The mother could angrily say, "Just do it—I'm not your servant!" That would be a simple, candid response, with a clear focus on the situation at hand. But suppose the incident symbolizes many other hurts: lack of appreciation from her husband, frustration at not having time for herself, and even guilt because she doesn't do enough for her family. If the mother's reaction is propelled by all that extra fuel, it will be much stronger. She might drag in other issues or exaggerate the daughter's offense ("You never help! You're totally selfish—you don't care about me at all!"); she could completely lose her temper or impose a punishment out of proportion to the offense.

There's no clear-cut boundary between expression of feelings and ventilation, between having a strong reaction and throwing a temper tantrum. So how can you tell that you're slipping over the edge? Here are a few guidelines:

- Straightforward expressions of feelings, because they reflect reality, usually seem understandable; ventilation is more likely to be exaggerated and incomprehensible. Listen for words like "Always" and "Never"—they usually signal ventilation.
- Ventilation is more likely to include extraneous issues—not just the current incident, but events from long ago. One phrase that should raise a red flag is: "This is just another example . . ."
- The person toward whom a ventilating response is addressed may feel attacked and say things like: "You're overreacting" or "This comes out of the blue." If it's a child, she might burst into tears or act fearful.

Though it's best to express emotions honestly and directly, nearly everyone blows up occasionally. Indeed, you may decide in retrospect that an outburst was helpful, if it focused attention on previously ignored problems and energized family efforts to change. But explosions should be the exception. Children are not harmed by an occasional episode of parental irrationality. However, they are adversely affected if it becomes a frequent occurrence. When a youngster says, "My mommy is always angry," or "I'm scared of my father," she's virtually never talking about a single incident, but a pattern.

What if your partner is venting, and you're the recipient? I often compare ventilation to a storm and suggest that the best reaction is to allow it to run its course. It's not easy! If someone is attacking, your natural impulse is to defend yourself. When your spouse is being unfair or unreasonable, you want to set the record straight. Your own passions may be stirred by what they're saying or doing. But the storm will do far more damage if you add your energy to it.

Try very hard to remain calm if you find yourself in this situation. Suspend judgment. Not participating is the most effective way to bring the episode to a close. Once the storm has passed, you can move on to a more constructive discussion of feelings. At that point you can ask questions, encourage your partner to speak, and voice your sympathy, concern, and support.

RESPONDING TO YOUR CHILD'S FEELINGS

Children are even more likely than adults to express feelings strongly and irrationally: They have less self-understanding and less control. Here too, the ideal response is to listen and be as neutral as possible. Later, when the storm has passed, you can return to the substantive issues and deal with them.

As with a spouse, this is easier said than done! Often, when a child is venting, *you* are the target—and it's difficult to remain calm when you're under attack. Make a strong effort not to be personally affected by it, even if your child screams, "I hate you!" in a furious moment. If the youngster goes too far—for example, if she uses forbidden language or throws something—you certainly can stop her with a firm, "You can tell me you're angry, but swearing is not allowed!" But avoid getting carried away and sinking to her level.

Another common parental reaction to the child's strong feelings— one that grows out of a desire to help—is moving in too quickly with a logical response. No sooner does the youngster begin to express her feelings than the parents jump to the next step and cut her off. If there's a problem, they try to solve it; if the child is upset, they reassure; if the youngster's outpouring is irrational, they make corrections. But the best response when a child ventilates is simply to listen.

Twelve-year-old Maria is an example. She's unhappy with her Italian grandmother, who is spending the summer with the family, supervising Maria while her mother is at work. Maria complains that her grandmother is invading her privacy; she listens in on telephone conversations and reads Maria's mail. Her mother, who is the daughter-in-law of this woman, knows exactly what Maria is talking about. So she tries to help by explaining the cultural reasons for the grandmother's behavior. But Maria simply gets angrier, and her complaints become more unreasonable.

What Maria's mother might do instead is listen to the complaints and acknowledge that the grandmother *is* intrusive. If Maria makes extraneous hostile remarks, her mother can ignore them. She can close the conversation by saying, "Let's talk again later." When Maria's anger has dissipated, she will be more receptive to her mother's explanations. In fact, she herself may point out that the problem is partly cultural.

Usually ventilation ends on its own: The youngster expresses her feelings, runs out of steam, and stops. But some persistent children get stuck instead of winding down. If this happens with your child, don't get angry; just bring the discussion to an end as quickly as possible. Exactly how you do that depends on the individual child. You could offer a distraction, ignore the outburst, firmly tell her to stop, or leave the room.

ENCOURAGING YOUR CHILD TO TALK

Displays of emotion, however excessive, at least let you know that your child is upset—and may even provide clues about the reason. Far more frustrating is the situation in which a youngster seems to be in distress, but refuses to talk about it. You want so very much to help, but you're rebuffed with silence or a stoical, "I'm okay—just leave me alone."

One possibility is that there really isn't anything wrong. Until preadolescence, most youngsters have little interest in talking extensively about their feelings. Parents sometimes assume that superficial answers to their anxious questions mean that the child is concealing painful emotions. But they may be looking for something that simply isn't there. Few young children are deep and subtle.

Rafi is a good example. He has just started second grade and seems subdued. His mom is afraid that something at school is making him unhappy, so she questions him. If the dialogue sounds familiar, it's not surprising—this is a perfectly normal conversation for a seven-year-old:

"How did things go today?" the mother asks.

"Okay," says Rafi.

"Is your teacher nice?"

"She's okay."

"Do you like her?"

"Yeah."

"Do you like the other kids in your class?"

"Yeah. They're okay."

Sensitive parents, out of the best of motives, sometimes go too far and turn into "psychological dentists," attempting to extract feelings as if they were teeth. Children may experience this as intrusive and become even more resistant.

Or the parents may turn to verbal formulas intended to facilitate communication. For instance, they may repeat a child's statements to show they hear what he's saying. This can be helpful, because it reminds you to listen carefully; it also prevents you from rushing in with your own ideas. However, some children recoil when their parents parrot artificial-sounding canned phrases like "What I hear you saying is . . ."

You don't have to adopt a new personality or go out of your way to make therapeutic comments when you talk to your child. Instead:

- *Ask specific, concrete questions.* Rafi's mother could get past his vague answers, and learn about his day at school, with questions like these: Who sits at your lunch table? What are you learning in math? Who's on your soccer team?

- *Indicate a genuine willingness to listen.* Gail's mother is so eager to find out why her eight-year-old daughter came home from a play date in tears that she bombards the girl with questions: "What happened? Are you hurt? Who was there? Was someone mean?" If she gave Gail a chance to speak, she might find out!

Once Gail begins to describe the episode that upset her, she might need encouragement to continue. Her mother could say something like: "You've told me a little bit already, and I'm beginning to understand. Could you tell me some more?" She could praise her daughter's honesty with: "I know this is very hard to talk about; you're brave to tell me."

- *Consider less direct means of communication.* Some families find notes or letters effective with an older child. Or they use discussions about television programs, movies, or stories to broach a delicate subject. Many youngsters are very responsive to parents' accounts of similar experiences from their own childhoods.

GUIDELINES FOR A PLANNED DISCUSSION

Minor problems may resolve themselves if feelings are aired and acknowledged. But sometimes that's just the preliminary step, and a calm, rational talk is needed to go further.

Unlike an ordinary conversation, a planned discussion involves preparation and a commitment to maintain objectivity:

- *Make an appointment.* A planned discussion is scheduled in advance, because it requires preparation. You should be ready to put your feelings behind you and to think more objectively.
- *Plan for the meeting.* Give the situation preliminary thought and clarify your ideas as much as possible. An agenda will help you maintain your focus: It's easy for a discussion to ramble and miss important areas. You can work from a written plan, but it's not essential; just make sure all participants know ahead of time what's under discussion.
- *Adopt a collaborative attitude.* A planned discussion requires a new attitude. You and your spouse may have been blaming each other or the child; there may be anger and defensiveness. But now your aim is to join forces and approach the problem cooperatively.
- *Try to remain objective.* Expressing your feelings ahead of time

should help you approach the planned discussion with greater objectivity. In addition, you and your spouse might want to restate your
commitment to remain calm.

Parents sometimes express concern that such a degree of planning
will be artificial and diminish the spontaneity of family life. Remember,
however, that this is a specific technique used only to evaluate problems
or plan solutions. Though the formality may seem awkward at first,
most families quickly become used to it.

Depending upon the situation, the mother and father might have a
planned discussion with each other; afterward, they might use the
technique to talk to their child. The same method could be used for all-
family discussions when issues involve more than one child. Any youngster old enough to join a meaningful conversation can participate in a
planned discussion. Mothers and fathers in my practice have used them
successfully with children as young as three.

THE PLANNED DISCUSSION WITH YOUR SPOUSE

Your attitude—neutral and geared to problem solving—is the key to a
successful planned discussion. Realize that it won't be easy to maintain!
Everyone has a tendency to fall into old patterns, but recognizing this
should help you recover.

Kirsten's parents had a planned discussion about their daughter the
day after their fruitless confrontation with her. The talk between the two
of them was intended as a preliminary effort, aimed at preparing for a
discussion with Kirsten.

*Circumstances are more favorable this time. Kirsten is away at a
friend's house; the parents have enjoyed a peaceful lunch.*

*Kirsten's mother begins: "I'm glad we're doing this—I have no idea
why she's having so much trouble in school."*

"Maybe the teacher really is mean," suggests the father.

*"You can't believe that! Obviously Kirsten is doing things to provoke
her. You know how she is."*

"No, I don't know that. Why can't you admit that it could be partly the teacher's fault? You're always ready to point a finger at Kirsten."
The mother gets angry. She says, "Here we go again!"

The parents have strayed from the topic at hand—Kirsten's school problems—and have gotten into their issues with each other. When this happens in my office, I call a halt and urge both parents to pull back. If they don't, I may say pointedly: "You've paid me a lot of money for this evaluation, so why do you want to have the same kind of argument you can have at home for free?" Parents usually can learn to correct themselves once they become aware of what they are doing.

Kirsten's parents realize what's happening. They stop talking and compose themselves.
"I shouldn't have put it that way," says Kirsten's father. "But I think you ought to consider the possibility that this isn't all Kirsten's fault. You know, she's never before said that a teacher was mean."
Kirsten's mother thinks for a minute. "That's true. I'm going to a curriculum meeting at school next week. I could ask some of the other parents how their kids are doing."
"Good idea," says the father. "We also have to talk to Kirsten again, but this time we've got to bite our tongues and listen to what she has to say."
"I find it so hard to just sit there while she makes wild accusations!" says the mother. "But you're right. I'll make a big effort to keep quiet and let her talk. Stop me if I forget."

It is not easy to break long-established patterns, but Kirsten's parents have made a start. If you run into trouble and can't get back on track quickly, suspend the planned discussion—it won't work. Agree to resume later. Instead of being discouraged, you can congratulate yourself on stopping; that's a positive step.

Not all couples and families will be able to do this. There may be long-standing antagonisms, hostile patterns of relating, hidden agendas and alliances—all of which sabotage efforts at effective communication. If you find you aren't making progress, and that even with repeated efforts you can't talk about problems constructively, you might benefit from professional help.

THE PLANNED DISCUSSION WITH YOUR CHILD

When you're trying to understand a youngster's problems, it's usually essential to get his or her view of the situation. Your child has information that you don't and undoubtedly sees things differently from the way you do.

Children, like adults, should have a chance to prepare for a planned discussion. Make an appointment to meet; ask the child to think about the situation in the meantime. Assure him that he will be heard and his contribution will be valued.

At first, children may be reluctant to talk. The slightly formal atmosphere of a planned discussion is new to them; past experience with family arguments may have made them cautious. Youngsters may assume that even if their mother and father listen, they won't understand. Sometimes they're ashamed, or fear what their parents' reaction might be. If so, you can promise restraint: "I won't laugh" or "I'll try not to get angry" or "I'll really listen to you this time."

Don't expect the same kind of objectivity from a child that you can get from an adult. Until midadolescence, most youngsters aren't self-reflective or self-critical, especially if they're upset. So they may not recognize their own role in creating a problem.

You can see this with Abby, a bossy six-year-old girl who frequently criticizes other children. One day during art period at school, she makes a disparaging comment about a picture Maya is painting. Maya retaliates by scribbling on Abby's work; a messy paint fight ensues, and the teacher punishes both girls. When Abby's parents ask her about the incident she says indignantly, "Maya started! She messed my painting for no reason!" Abby isn't deliberately evading responsibility; she truly doesn't recognize her contribution to the episode.

Nevertheless, even young children often surprise their mothers and fathers with the new information they bring—especially about the parents' own behavior. That's what happened with Michael's mother. Her son was seven and spent alternate weekends at his father's apartment. Sunday evenings, when he returned to his mother, he was grumpy and demanding; he rudely rebuffed her when she tried to talk to him. She often wondered if his father had been criticizing her and stirring up trouble.

Instead of confronting Michael on a Sunday, she waited a few days, then scheduled a planned discussion for Wednesday evening. She asked him what had been going wrong. He told her: "When I come home, you start hugging and kissing me like I was a baby." He performed an exaggerated imitation.

His mother was surprised and hurt, but she simply said, "Thanks for telling me." Later, when Michael was in bed and she had time to think, she realized that his description of her behavior was basically accurate. The following Sunday, she greeted her son with a warm, "Welcome back!" and instead of hugging him, winked and offered a handshake. Michael rewarded her with an understanding laugh, and the rest of the evening went well.

Like any new way of doing things, the planned discussion will seem more natural as you and your family become accustomed to it. Over time and with practice, your ability to communicate about problems should improve greatly.

After one failed attempt, in which Kirsten's parents strayed into an argument with her, the family had their first satisfactory planned discussion:

Kirsten sits with her parents in the living room; she looks tense and wary.

Her mother starts: "When we've tried to talk like this before, it hasn't worked. It's not just because of you, and we're going to try to do it differently this time. Kirsten, we really want to help you with school. We're on your side. But we need to know more about what's going on. What is the problem?"

"I hate my teacher. She's so mean. I wish I didn't have to go to school," says Kirsten.

Her father says, "You've said before that she's mean. What exactly does she do—could you give me an example?"

"She yells at me in front of the whole class."

Her father asks specific, factual questions. "How often does she yell at you?"

"A lot."

"Well, is it every day?"

"Not every day, but most days. I'm always scared she's going to yell at me. And, she's not fair."

"Why do you say that?" asks her mother.

"Sometimes she yells at me when I haven't done anything. Like the other day, she thought I was talking but I wasn't. Then when I tried to explain, she said I was being fresh, and she yelled even more."

"That must have been very frustrating," her mother comments sympathetically. "Does she yell at other kids or just at you?"

"Sometimes it's other kids, but mainly it's me."

Kirsten's mother takes a deep breath. "Kirsten, I really don't want to sound critical, but do you think that maybe you're doing something that contributes to the problem?"

Kirsten remains calm; she thinks for a minute. "Well, I talk back. Other kids just ignore it when she's unfair."

"I guess you're trying to stand up for what's right, Kirsten," says her father.

"I really hate it when people aren't fair," says Kirsten.

Kirsten's school problems are far from over. But she and her parents have made important progress in this discussion. In addition to gaining specific information, they're learning to talk calmly and constructively.

■   ■   ■   ■

Don't expect family communication to be magically transformed by these changes. But if you take the first steps, you should see encouraging improvements. Parents who have had their first successful planned discussion—who are able to tackle a difficult issue in a family discussion, remain calm, and make some progress—are exhilarated. Often they are surprised but very happy to see that their child is making a real effort to cooperate with them. They come back and tell me, "It really worked!"

INTRODUCTION TO THE
PARENTAL EVALUATION

The Parental Evaluation, which is presented in the next three chapters of this book, guides you through a systematic examination of your child's situation. You will describe the problems; consider your child's personality and history; and review possibly relevant features of his home and school environments.

As you have seen in Chapter 3, my initial assessment of a child and family doesn't just gather information; it's also part of the intervention. Similarly, this evaluation is designed not only to marshal your parental knowledge, but also to foster new attitudes and approaches.

The evaluation should help you understand the problems and some of the factors behind them; what you learn will generate many positive ideas for change. By the time you finish the evaluation, you probably will know whether your changes will suffice, or if you're likely to need professional help. Apart from more specific measures, you should find that your view of the youngster has become more understanding and sympathetic. This attitudinal shift is a vital part of the solution, regardless of the nature of the problem.

A thorough evaluation requires a serious commitment from parents. Below are suggestions to help you plan the process so that you make the most of it.

FINDING THE TIME

Going through the next three chapters will require one or more planned discussions. I can't tell you exactly how long it will take or how many sessions will be needed, because that depends upon the complexity of your situation. Some parents will decide to perform the evaluation all at once; others will prefer to take breaks.

You'll do best if you're well-rested and clearheaded. It's helpful to turn off the telephone and shield yourself from other distractions. If you can't arrange for children to be elsewhere, hold the discussions when they're asleep. If the problems are serious, and there's no other opportunity to talk, consider hiring a sitter or even staying home from work.

Parents are sometimes taken aback when I make these suggestions. Jamie's mother and father obviously love their eight-year-old daughter, who is very unhappy and falling behind in school. They had told me that they would "do anything" for her, but when I recommended that they take a day off from work to discuss the situation, it became clear that they needed to think more flexibly:

> MOTHER: *I couldn't possibly take time off from my job! Other people at the office count on me.*
> ST: *You certainly have important responsibilities, but earlier you said that you've been distracted at work for weeks worrying about your daughter, and that's a far more harmful disruption.*
> FATHER: *It's not realistic—I simply don't have that kind of time.*
> ST: *I realize that this sounds very demanding to you, but I'm not really suggesting that you spend more time. You've already told me that you and your wife talk about your daughter "endlessly." Having a thorough discussion about the situation won't add to that. Indeed, it should help you become more focused and efficient.*
> MOTHER: *Well, we'll think about it.*
> ST: *I suggest you keep track of how much nonproductive time Jamie's problems consume. Then, when the two of you next find yourselves talking about her, break off and schedule a more systematic discussion.*

WHAT IF YOUR SPOUSE WON'T HELP?

Ideally, if the child lives with two parents, both should participate: Her problems are a family issue. (Incidentally, I use the word "parents" to mean the adults with whom the youngster lives most of the time, not necessarily her biological mother and father.) It's important to approach the reluctant partner in a serious, well-thought-out way. If this doesn't work, start the evaluation on your own and share the ideas you develop: They are the most convincing proof that the effort is worthwhile. If all your attempts at persuasion fail, do the evaluation yourself.

DEALING WITH AN EX

Communicating with your child's other parent is especially difficult if the two of you are in conflict. But you may need his or her cooperation and input, even if you're no longer a couple. When I'm consulted by divorced parents, the best advice I can give them is to try their very best to maintain a focus on the needs of their child. That means making a strong effort to communicate neutrally and to separate their issues with each other from those involving the youngster.

I don't minimize the difficulty of doing this—especially if the breakup of the relationship is ongoing or recent. Sometimes estranged parents are more successful at communicating in writing. Ex-partners can't always work around the personal issues between them, and the custodial parent may have to do the evaluation alone. If discussion and shared decision making are essential—as would be true for a divorced couple with joint custody—and ex-spouses find they cannot talk about issues productively, professional assistance is advisable.

WORKING SOLO

If you're a single parent, you probably know your child intimately. But the closeness between you also means that it's harder to separate your personal issues from those of the youngster. Soliciting ideas from adults who know your family can be very helpful when you don't have the second opinion of a spouse.

GETTING INPUT FROM OTHERS

Whether or not you're working alone, it can be useful to consult other people during the evaluation. Listen carefully to their views, even if your first reaction is that they're off base.

■ A teacher can describe your child's behavior and relationships in school.

■ The child's doctor can provide information about normal development and tell you how your son or daughter compares to others the same age.

■ A noncustodial stepparent, if he or she knows your child well, could contribute an intimate but more objective view.

■ Friends and relatives might have useful insights.

■ Acquaintances who see your child when you're not around—such as scoutmasters and parents of playmates—sometimes can provide helpful information.

■   ■   ■   ■

Performing the evaluation gives most parents a sense of mastery. I hope you also will feel more confident and in control as you take an organized, objective approach to what probably had been fragmentary impressions colored by anxiety.

FIVE

YOUR CHILD'S PROBLEMS

When I ask parents what has brought them to my office, they often tell me of some "last straw": an experience with their child that crystalized their worries and frustration.

>   *"Our nine-year-old son was suspended from school for pushing his teacher."*
>   *"I was at the mall with my five-year-old daughter, and she kept running off. The third time she did it, something snapped, and I slapped her. She screamed bloody murder, and the next thing I knew, there was this cop asking questions like my kid was an abused child."*
>   *"I've been worried because my twelve-year-old daughter seems sad, but now I'm petrified. Look at the last line of this poem she wrote: 'Death, I embrace you.' "*

In other cases, the parents come to me because of long-standing concerns.

"She's impossible! She won't do her homework, won't finish her chores, won't do anything I say. Everything turns into an argument or a debate. You never saw such an expert negotiator."

"My son doesn't seem to like himself. He'll say things like, 'I'm stupid' or 'I'm no good' or 'I'm a bad boy.' If he makes a mistake, he bursts into tears. He's a real perfectionist."

"My daughter is in her own world most of the time. Her teacher says she doesn't pay attention in class, and her grades are terrible. She's become moody, and she's lost her sparkle."

"He's always moving around and touching things. He can't sit still for a minute. It drives me crazy at home, and I get constant complaints from the school about him disrupting the class."

"My kid is a nervous wreck. When I finally got him to stop biting his nails, he started twirling his hair. He's scared of the dark and insists on going to sleep with all the lights on."

Wherever you start—with a specific incident, a long list of complaints, a particular worry, a warning from a teacher, or just a vague sense that something is wrong—it helps to think about the difficulties in a systematic way. This chapter will guide you through an assessment of your child's problems. By the end, you will have specific, concise descriptions of the particular problems that concern you the most.

The issue may involve behavior that frustrates or annoys you; or the youngster's symptoms may seem to be outside her control, so that you're worried rather than angry. In either case, you should find it helpful to step back and take a more objective look.

WHAT ARE YOUR CONCERNS?

Your initial answer may be an outpouring that contains much more than information about problems. With the mother of six-year-old Nathan, the question opens a floodgate. As you read her response, be aware of the many directions it takes. Intermingled with her description of Nathan's current problems are her anxious speculations about possible causes, comments about his temperament, expressions of frustration, descriptions of her efforts at discipline, feelings about her husband, and memories of her childhood:

> *Where do I begin? Nathan has always been stubborn* [temperament], *but since he started school, it's been worse than ever. Sometimes I'm ready to walk out. There's always a big argument: I can't get him to do anything* [mother's frustration]. *If I tell him to get dressed in the morning or brush his teeth at night, he refuses. When I insist, he gets angry and calls me names* [current problem].
>
> *I've tried everything. In the beginning, I would reason with him, but that didn't work. I've threatened and punished him every way I can think of* [efforts at discipline]. *Sometimes I just cave in and let him do what he wants. I'm also worried because he seems unhappy all the time. He cries easily. A couple of times he's said that he's too sad to go to school* [current problems].
>
> *My husband is no help at all, totally unsupportive. I'm furious with him: He doesn't lift a finger, but he's always ready to criticize what I'm doing. He undermines me when I try to lay down the law with Nathan* [feelings about husband]. *I can't believe that one child could be so much trouble. There were five of us when I was growing up, and in a month my mom didn't raise her voice as often as I do every day* [memories of childhood].
>
> *I keep wondering if we did the right thing by letting him start first grade this year. His birthday is just before the cut-off date, and his kindergarten teacher warned us he was immature. But he was already reading—he's very bright—and we didn't see keeping him back. I don't know if he's under too much pressure, or what the problem is* [speculations about the possible cause].

It's only natural for worried parents to be thinking about many issues. Nathan's mother has mentioned several factors that may be contributing to the difficulties, including her husband's behavior and the boy's school situation. These should not be forgotten. But at this stage, she simply needs to list Nathan's problems. When we put aside everything else in her statement, what's left is much briefer and more focused: Nathan is stubborn and argumentative; he won't get dressed or brush his teeth; he doesn't obey his mother; he gets angry and calls her names; he seems unhappy and says he's sad; and he cries easily.

Some parents find it helpful to write down the problems; others are content with a mental list. Either way, try to be comprehensive. Parents almost always notice difficulties that put the youngster in conflict with others or interfere with his functioning: If a boy is too scared to go to bed by himself, or if he's aggressive, demanding, and uncooperative, they can hardly fail to see it. But sometimes the issues are less obvious.

An unhappy youngster may not be weepy—any parent would be aware of that; instead, she may express her sadness by becoming unusually quiet or preoccupied. Be aware of persistent changes that are out of the ordinary, including physical changes: Frequent headaches or stomachaches can be unrecognized signs of emotional distress.

In the case of Olga, age eleven, a serious but more subtle problem initially was obscured by one dramatic episode: She was caught shoplifting in a department store by the security guard, and her parents were summoned to take her home. Understandably, their first reaction was anger. Initially, they focused on devising a suitable punishment: Olga was grounded for several weeks and required to write a letter of apology to the store owner.

During the days that followed, the parents continued to talk about their daughter's problems, and they realized in retrospect that she had been showing signs of distress for about six months. Her school grades were slipping, and she seemed mopey, pessimistic, and distracted. Instead of getting together with friends on weekends, she'd been sleeping and watching TV a lot. "Typical preteen behavior," their friends had told them. But with this incident, that explanation no longer satisfied them. They decided they needed a professional evaluation and came to me. I recognized a mild depression and suggested several measures, including therapy and some changes in Olga's program at school.

IS SELF-IMAGE A FACTOR?

When I evaluate a youngster, I pay a great deal of attention to self-image. If a child has a basically positive self-image, I'm always optimistic about the outcome.

As a parent, you can't probe directly, as a psychiatrist would, to assess self-image. However, you sometimes can detect self-image problems by what the youngster says or does. Cherilyn, age nine, never raises her hand at school. "I'm dumb," she says. "I never know the answers." She berates herself when she drops a glass: "I'm so clumsy. I can't do anything right!" Such statements should not be overinterpreted if they're said only in moments of anger or emotional distress. But they are cause for concern if they seem to reflect the youngster's consistent view of herself.

Here are more indirect indicators of a poor self-image:

- *Hypersensitivity to criticism or failure.* Hiroshi becomes so upset when he makes a mistake that his parents hesitate to correct him.
- *Cheating at games or being a sore loser.* In a school-age child, inability to accept defeat usually indicates that the youngster's self-esteem is on the line even in a game.
- *Bragging and demanding attention.* Most people don't realize that Dominique lacks self-confidence because she constantly boasts and shows off. But if she really felt good about herself, she wouldn't need to do this.
- *Bullying and victim behavior.* Whenever George ventures into the neighborhood playground, Marty threatens to beat him up. Though George always retreats, he keeps returning and continues to seek Marty out. Despite the striking difference in their behavior, the boys are two sides of the same coin. A child who lacks confidence may pick on other kids—or set himself up to be the target of bullies.
- *Trying too hard to attract friends.* Suki, age eight, is the class clown. She's so eager for the applause of her classmates that she is willing to risk getting into trouble.

The natural response of parents, when a youngster seems down on herself, is to try to boost her self-image with exaggerated praise. They say things like, "You're wonderful!" or "That's the best painting I ever saw—it should be in a museum!" However, impaired self-image is never a problem on its own, and parents can't address it directly. A negative self-image is always an outgrowth of other problems, such as a poor fit at school or inappropriate expectations at home. When these difficulties are corrected, self-image often improves automatically.

However, sometimes self-image problems take on a life of their own. The youngster's negative opinion of himself persists despite what is actually happening in his life: In the friendliest environment, he feels unaccepted; no matter how successful he is in the eyes of others, he's not satisfied with himself. Such a situation requires professional help.

DECIDE WHERE TO START

At this point, you have a mental or written list of your child's problems. If you're like Nathan's mother, some items may be relatively minor and simple (Nathan won't brush his teeth without a struggle), while others are more serious and complex (Nathan is disobedient and sad).

Agreeing on priorities will help you and your spouse focus your efforts to help your child. Concentrating on a few issues increases your chance of success—it's simply not possible to deal with too much at once. You aren't giving up on other areas, just putting them aside for a while. When you return to them, you may be pleasantly surprised. Parents often find that success breeds success: When they overcome one problem, others disappear on their own. If that doesn't happen, any remaining difficulties can be dealt with later.

Here are some guidelines for choosing where to start:

- *The problem interferes with the child's functioning.* If your daughter's bossiness has caused several of her favorite playmates to back off, and she's clearly unhappy about that, it's an important problem. But if the issue is only that *you* don't care for her imperious style, it can wait.
- *The problem is a recurring one.* If you've seen the difficulty be-

fore, or if it comes up in several settings, it isn't likely to disappear on its own. If your son didn't make friends in the summer day camp he attended when he was eight, you may have decided that the group wasn't congenial, or that the counselor didn't do enough to bring the children together. But if the same thing also happens at school and in his scout troop, you need to address the issue.

▪ *Both parents are distressed.* Sometimes parents view a specific problem differently. The orderly father of a disorganized ten-year-old boy may see sloppiness as a significant liability; but his mother, though she also would like her son to be neater, gives this issue low priority. If you and your spouse agree about the need to address a problem, it probably deserves your attention.

▪ *The child is upset about the problem.* Certain difficulties loom larger to a child than to an adult, and vice versa. You may not be distressed that your seven-year-old son still wets his bed occasionally at night, and he may not care either. If so, it can wait. But if he unhappily turns down slumber-party invitations because he doesn't want friends to discover his secret, the problem merits attention. It's best not to assume you know how he feels; a planned discussion is a good way to solicit his views.

▪ *A person whose judgment you respect expresses concern.* Don't panic just because a teacher, a doctor, or an experienced parent says that something is wrong. But the comment certainly merits weight, especially if this is a person whose knowledge and judgment you respect.

Supportive parents may minimize problems because they don't want their child to feel bad. Or they may fear others will label the youngster. I refer to reactions like these as **loving denial.** While the intent is clearly positive, the effect may be counter productive. Howard's mother and father downplayed warnings from his second-grade teacher that he was struggling academically. Only months later, after Howard had become moody and withdrawn, were they willing to acknowledge that he needed help. A subsequent evaluation revealed a learning disability.

DESCRIBE THE PROBLEMS OBJECTIVELY

Your goal is to come up with a brief, almost clinical description of each problem. This is not merely an exercise in language! When you're able to see separate, clearly defined elements, difficulties will seem far more manageable.

Here are two examples from my practice that show how I questioned mothers to convert vague initial statements into something far more specific and useful. The first mom began by telling me that her six-year-old son is aggressive.

ST: *With whom is your son aggressive?*

MOTHER: *With other children.*

ST: *What exactly does he do to them?*

MOTHER: *He hits and pushes.*

ST: *Has he ever seriously hurt another child?*

MOTHER: *Only once. He didn't mean to—the boy fell and scraped his arm.*

ST: *Where do these episodes occur?*

MOTHER: *In the neighborhood playground. I've gotten complaints about him from other parents.*

ST: *Is he aggressive at school?*

MOTHER: *I don't think so. They would have called me if he'd done that.*

ST: *What about with his siblings?*

MOTHER: *Not really. He and his older sister get into arguments sometimes, but he's never hit her.*

ST: *How often does he hit children in the playground?*

MOTHER: *It varies.*

ST: *Pick an average.*

MOTHER: *Maybe once or twice a week.*

ST: *How long has he been doing this?*

MOTHER: *It's hard to say.*

ST: *Well, how long has it been a real concern for you?*

MOTHER: *He's always been rough. But the hitting started just in the past month.*

"He's aggressive" has now become "He has been hitting and pushing other children in the neighborhood playground once or twice a week for the past month, but has never seriously hurt anyone."

In the second case, the mother was worried about her nine-year-old daughter. Among other things, she told me that the girl had no friends.

> ST: *When you say she has no friends, do you mean that literally?*
>
> MOTHER: *No, not literally. There's one girl who's been her best friend since second grade. And there are two others she sees occasionally.*
>
> ST: *Does she complain or seem upset because she isn't more popular?*
>
> MOTHER: *She hasn't said anything. But it's not normal for a girl that age to spend so much time with just one friend.*
>
> ST: *What's relevant isn't what other children do, but what's normal for your daughter. Looking back at previous years, has she generally had a lot of friends, or just a few?*
>
> MOTHER: *No—it's always been this way. When she was little, I tried to help her broaden her circle, but she would insist on playing with the same few kids all the time.*
>
> ST: *Is it possible that your daughter is simply the kind of person who prefers to have one or two close friends rather than being popular with a larger group?*
>
> MOTHER: (Laughs) *You're saying what she says—that it's my problem, not hers.*

By taking a much closer and more objective look at the statement "My daughter has no friends," the mother realizes that her daughter isn't really socially isolated. Moreover, she understands that the current situation, which is consistent with past patterns, may reflect the girl's true preferences rather than an emotional difficulty.

What I'm trying to learn when I question parents this way is the severity, frequency, duration, and setting of a problem. You and your spouse can use the questions on the next page to construct a full description of each problem:

■ *How severe is the problem?* Severity refers to the impact of a problem on the functioning of the child and on others in his environment. One way to describe severity is to put each issue on a spectrum and imagine the extremes; then you can place the child somewhere in between.

A spectrum of aggression could cover this range:

> (*Mild*) Verbal aggression
> (*Moderate*) Hitting and pushing without injuring
> (*Severe*) Inflicting pain or injury on others

A similar spectrum for social inhibition would be:

> (*Mild*) Becoming disinterested in friends
> (*Moderate*) Relationships limited to family members
> (*Severe*) Withdrawal from all social contact

If the problem is defiance, annoying verbal protests would be at the mild end of the range; at the severe end would be very disruptive defiance—say, a junior high school student who curses at his teachers during class and openly refuses to obey them. Test anxiety could span a spectrum from a smiling admission of nervousness to extreme tension with such physical manifestations as nausea and trembling.

■ *How frequent is the problem?* A youngster might have two serious temper tantrums a day, or approximately one a week; a girl might annoy her older sister nearly every time they're together, or just on relatively infrequent occasions when she's upset. Be as specific as possible in describing frequency.

■ *What is the duration of the problem?* In other words, how long has the child experienced this difficulty? If you aren't sure because it built up gradually, try to remember when you first became concerned. Pinpointing when a problem began can help identify the cause. If it's always been an issue, that's a clue that you may be dealing with temperament or a more deeply ingrained problem. Recent problems may reflect a developmental stage, or a reaction to a new stress.

■ *In what settings does the problem occur?* Setting means circumstances, places, and individuals. Consider all the places in which your child functions and all the people with whom she interacts. This could include the home (mother, father, siblings, and babysitter); school (teachers, peers); camp and other organized activities (leaders; other participants); extended family (grandparents, other adults, children); neighborhood (adults, older and younger children); and any other settings.

Are there circumstances in which the problem is absent, or is it always evident? For example, your daughter may be extremely argumentative with you, but not with her teacher or your spouse. This will direct attention toward your relationship with her as a possible factor in the problem.

■   ■   ■   ■

You now have identified and described your child's most pressing problems. In the process, I hope you also have learned how much it helps to examine troubling issues more objectively and systematically. By this point you and your spouse may have concluded—as Olga's parents did when they realized that their daughter's shoplifting was part of a more extensive problem—that you need professional assistance. If so, Chapter 12 can provide further guidance.

Chapter 6 will help you take a thorough look at your child's temperament, development, and personal history. This will enable you to view the issues you've just identified in the context of his or her normal self.

SIX

YOUR CHILD'S NORMAL SELF

This chapter asks you to look at the essence of your child's personality when there are no special problems. The present difficulties must be viewed against this baseline: "Normal" means different things for different children.

As I explained in Chapter 2, the characteristics that comprise a child's normal self have a strong innate component. These built-in elements are the framework that shapes personality. But this structure is made of the psychic equivalent of pliable plastic rather than steel rods: The child's normal self sets limits on what can realistically be expected; however, the framework is not rigid and can be molded by outside influences. Biology is *not* destiny!

Certain characteristics or stressful past experiences may make a youngster vulnerable to emotional problems. These are risk factors that you need to take into account. Sometimes mothers and fathers fear that a youngster who is at risk is doomed to a lifetime of problems. They anxiously link every difficulty to a troubling characteristic or a worrisome feature of the youngster's history. Yet, as I constantly remind parents, awareness of your child's special sensitivities should be balanced by an appreciation of her strengths, including her resilience.

I hope you will approach the questions below in an optimistic spirit. Taking stock of your child's normal self will help you accept him and form appropriate expectations. You cannot expect to change who he is. However, if you recognize both his strengths and areas of vulnerability, you will understand him better and guide him more effectively.

DESCRIBE YOUR CHILD'S TEMPERAMENT

Temperamental characteristics are inborn personality traits. Though they can be modified by the youngster's environment as he grows and develops, they continue to affect how he feels and acts. Understanding your child's temperament can help you answer questions like these:

- *Is he having problems—or is he just being himself?* Certain temperamental traits may be mistaken for emotional problems by people who aren't familiar with the child's normal behavior and personality. Nearly every September, Gregory's new teacher calls his parents to express concern about the boy's apparent unhappiness in school. But Gregory's parents know that their nine-year-old son normally takes a long time to warm up in new situations. Though they provide extra support as he readjusts to being in school, they don't worry about him.

- *Is she doing this on purpose?* Vera's mother used to feel insulted when her seven-year-old daughter refused to eat food that wasn't perfectly cooked, such as slightly overdone toast. But this sensitivity was not new. Even as an infant, Vera had responded strongly to slight variations in taste. When Vera's mother could see her daughter's fussiness about food as a temperamental issue, and not as a deliberate effort to annoy her, her anger disappeared. She was able to accommodate Vera's preferences without taking them personally.

- *How seriously should you take the behavior?* Temperamental traits often become exaggerated when a youngster is under stress: A rough-tough kid may become aggressive; a child who usually is fussy about food may develop a whole new set of dislikes. Charlotte is a loud, flamboyant ten-year-old, given to melodramatic exaggeration. When she's upset, she says things like, "I *hate* you! I wish I was dead!" Her parents shouldn't ignore her distress. But they don't have to take her statements so literally that they rush her to a psychiatric emergency room.

Use the following table to describe your child's temperament. This list is more extensive than the one I offered in *The Difficult Child.* I have discovered in working with families that it is useful to view temperament more broadly. The point is to look for distinctive, stable features of her personality, which have been present since an early age and are evident in many settings. That implies they are innate, at least to some extent. As you will see, each characteristic covers a range. At one end are qualities that make a child easy to deal with; these are strengths of her personality. At the other extreme are difficult traits that may create conflict between the child and those around her; these are potential risk factors.

TEMPERAMENTAL CHARACTERISTIC	EASY (POTENTIAL ASSET)	DIFFICULT (POTENTIAL LIABILITY)
PREDOMINANT MOOD	Cheerful "We call him Mr. Sunshine." "She's always looking on the bright side."	Gloomy "He's a brooder and a moper." "She never cracks a smile."
DISPOSITION	Calm "Nothing fazes him." "She's always relaxed, even in tight situations."	High-strung "He's a worrywart." "He's always tense."

TEMPERAMENTAL CHARACTERISTIC	EASY (POTENTIAL ASSET)	DIFFICULT (POTENTIAL LIABILITY)
CONSISTENCY OF MOOD	Stable "He's steady and even-tempered."	Changeable, moody "He'll be just fine, and then suddenly something snaps." "He has good and bad days for no reason."
EMOTIONAL SENSITIVITY	Low "She takes things in her stride."	High "His feelings are very easily hurt." "She cries over everything."
SOCIABILITY	Outgoing "He makes new friends everywhere he goes."	Shy, timid "People think she's rude because she won't say hello." "He doesn't join in at birthday parties."
EXPRESSIVENESS	Expressive "She's very demonstrative."	Reserved, taciturn "You never know how he feels."
INITIAL RESPONSE	Approach "She loves to meet new people."	Withdrawal "New situations throw him."
EXPRESSION OF ANGER	Slow to anger "You can't get a rise out of her."	Hot-tempered "The slightest thing sets him off." "She has an extremely short fuse."

TEMPERAMENTAL CHARACTERISTIC	EASY (POTENTIAL ASSET)	DIFFICULT (POTENTIAL LIABILITY)
SELF-CONTROL	Deliberate "She tends to be thoughtful about what she does." "He's very patient."	Impulsive "He's always interrupting." "He acts before he thinks."
INTENSITY	Low-keyed "He's quiet and laid-back."	Loud, forceful "His personality is overwhelming." "You can hear him when you're two blocks away."
ACTIVITY LEVEL	Low to moderate "She's slow-moving." "He can sit quietly for a long time."	Very high "I wonder if he's hyperactive." "He's got ants in his pants, can't sit still." "She exhausts me—she's always on the go."
CONCENTRA-TION	Focused; long attention span "When you talk to her, she's right there."	Distractible; short attention span "He tunes you out." "She's forgetful and disorganized."
REGULARITY (OF SLEEPING AND EATING RHYTHMS)	Regular "You can set your clock by him."	Irregular "You can never predict when she'll be sleepy or hungry."

TEMPERAMENTAL CHARACTERISTIC	EASY (POTENTIAL ASSET)	DIFFICULT (POTENTIAL LIABILITY)
ADAPTABILITY TO CHANGE	Good; makes transitions easily "He goes with the flow."	Poor; is upset by transitions "She's very rigid." "He can't switch gears."
SENSORY THRESHOLD (TO LIGHT, TOUCH, TASTE, SMELL, AND SOUND)	High "He can sleep through anything."	Low "Bright lights really bother him." "She's always complaining that her clothes itch."
PREFERENCES (IN CLOTHING AND FOOD)	Flexible "She eats anything." "He doesn't care what he wears."	Particular, strong preferences "The world's pickiest eater." "Finding clothes she likes is a nightmare."
NEGATIVE PERSISTENCE	Cooperative, malleable "She knows when to stop."	Stubborn, resistant "He wears you down." "When she wants something, she never gives up."
POSITIVE PERSISTENCE	Goal focused "He sticks to the job until it's done."	Gives up easily "He starts, but he doesn't finish."

Not all children described as "difficult" are equally hard to raise. A hot-tempered child may have three or four verbal outbursts a month—or become extremely angry several times a day. A shy youngster may need a few minutes to warm up to new people—or refuse contact with anyone outside her family.

Many youngsters have a few difficult characteristics. Their significance depends a great deal on the fit between the child and his surroundings. Suppose a boy is inflexible and adjusts poorly to change. He could function very well in a family whose life and routines are firmly established. But the same youngster would have more trouble if his mother was a private nurse and his father was a fireman, and their irregular work schedules made for chronic unpredictability at home.

Sometimes an individual who is temperamentally difficult in one area is easy in others. I've observed that hot-tempered, hyperactive children, who are disruptive, impulsive, and distractible, almost inevitably are also funny, friendly, and open to new experiences. Often very shy children, who withdraw from new situations, can concentrate well and are predictable with regard to eating and sleeping.

The more difficult traits a child has, and the more severe they are, the greater the risk of conflict. For some extremely difficult youngsters, the fit would be poor in nearly any environment. Parents of such a child will have to make a considerable effort to manage him successfully.

CONSIDER YOUR CHILD'S DEVELOPMENT

We all know how much children change as they move from infancy through childhood and into adolescence. The milestones involve emotions and behavior, as well as physical growth. That's why you need to consider a youngster's age and developmental stage when evaluating a problem.

Development is only partly predictable, and so-called "norms" are merely averages. Just as babies seldom arrive on their due dates, few children are exactly on schedule developmentally. What's more, a child doesn't always develop at the same pace on all fronts: A youngster whose physical growth is relatively slow could be more socially mature than average; an intellectually precocious child might lag behind peers emotionally.

Developmental variation among different youngsters of the same age increases as children get older, because so many other factors are at work. For example, cognitive development could be encouraged—or stalled—by educational opportunities; the normal movement to independence from parents could be fostered by positive experiences with other children, or delayed by adverse circumstances such as prolonged illness.

Like temperament, a child's developmental pace and sequence are part of his normal self, an individual baseline against which his behavior can be evaluated. Below are questions to consider:

WHAT HAS BEEN THE PACE OF DEVELOPMENT?

Has your child generally reached milestones as expected—or has he been earlier or later than average? The youngster whose development is atypical may be subject to inappropriate expectations. When he repeatedly fails to meet the demands of others, he may come to believe that something is wrong with him. This is just as true if he's far ahead of his peers as when he's considerably behind them.

If this is your first child, or if you don't have much contact with other youngsters the same age, you may want to seek information from books, your child's doctor or teacher, or experienced parents. But general knowledge about development must be balanced with an awareness that your child follows his own blueprint.

Here's an example: There would be little cause for concern if a four-year-old cried and clung to his mother during the first week of nursery school—that's normal. But if a seven-year-old had a similar reaction to second grade, you would want to consider his developmental history. This is not a normal reaction for a youngster who is usually independent, and it would warrant prompt investigation. However, if this was a child whose emotional and social development has been consistently slower than average, separation problems at age seven might be normal *for him*. This is not to say that his parents should ignore the situation! But they and the teacher could simply give him extra support and adopt a wait-and-see attitude for a week or two.

Sometimes parents are overly concerned by minor deviations from average in their child's development: They worry if their one-year-old hasn't said her first word yet; if their four-year-old still wets the bed at night; or if their seven-year-old hasn't lost his babyish lisp. Of course, you don't want to go to the other extreme and be so unconcerned that you miss a real problem—so how do you strike a balance?

- Give weight to the opinions of those who have a lot of experience with children. Your child's physician or teacher is usually a good source of developmental information.
- Don't overcompare your child to others. In some communities, children are under a lot of pressure to grow up quickly, and a late-blooming youngster may seem deficient. If your child is thriving and functioning well, try not to worry about comments like: "His cousin was riding a two-wheeler by this age," or "Isn't she interested in boys yet?"
- Focus first on simple measures if you suspect an issue is developmental. If your child temporarily needs help to keep up with classmates, arrange for tutoring to see if that's enough. If you're looking for a camp for a ten-year-old who is still more girl than young woman, find a program where she would be grouped with nine-year-olds rather than elevens.

IS YOUR CHILD'S DEVELOPMENT UNEVEN?

Uneven development increases the risk that a child will be subject to inappropriate expectations. You probably have met youngsters who are advanced verbally but have poor motor skills—or vice versa. One pattern I see often is a combination of intellectual precocity and social or emotional immaturity. Adults make the understandable—but incorrect—assumption that a youngster who is highly verbal, or who displays excellent reasoning ability, is similarly mature in noncognitive areas. This is the kind of child about whom exasperated teachers and parents say: "If he's so bright, why doesn't he know how to control himself?" Here are two parents' descriptions of problems resulting from atypical development:

Kareem's teacher thinks he should repeat kindergarten because he hasn't learned his letters yet. She has a point, but it's not that simple. In most ways, he's mature for a six-year-old, so I'm afraid he'll feel out of place in kindergarten next year. The kids will seem too babyish; all of his friends are his own age or older. Also, he's very big for his age and good in sports, so he would stand out like a sore thumb in gym and recess.

Kareem is physically advanced, of at least normal social maturity, but cognitively behind his peers. He could enter first grade with a plan for extra support in academic areas, such as private tutoring in reading.

Betsy's problem is that she's too smart. I know that sounds weird, but let me tell you, it's no picnic. Her mental development was very precocious, and it's always been hard for her to relate to other kids her age. She spoke in complete sentences before she was two, and she would run up to other toddlers and ask them, "Can you talk yet?" Most of her friends are two or three years older than she is, and I don't know what she'll do when they hit adolescence.

Betsy's cognitive abilities are advanced, but otherwise her development is average. She might need two sets of friends—some at her mental level, and others of her chronological age.

Is Your Child Going Through a Stage?

Certain emotional and behavioral problems reflect developmental phases and should be recognized as such. For example, parents probably don't have to look beyond development to explain why a preschooler is afraid of dogs, or a five-year-old is experimenting with bathroom language. And if your twelve-year-old daughter becomes moody and weepy for no apparent reason, puberty is a prime suspect. Such phases may require extra parental understanding and support, but they can be expected to pass without special intervention.

Developmental progress is not necessarily smooth. Children go through spurts, followed by periods of consolidation in which they may appear not to change, or even to regress. For instance, a six-year-old might act very independent and insist upon going on sleepovers—and then during the next month he might become clingy and babyish.

How do you know that a problem simply represents a normal

regression or a predictable developmental stage, and not something more serious? Generally, the behavior will be new, relatively mild, and temporary; there will be no obvious other cause for it. You may have had a preview from other parents, or recognize the same pattern from other youngsters. If you're unsure, ask your child's doctor or teacher if what you're seeing is typical for that age.

ARE THERE ANY SPECIAL RISK FACTORS?

We've already seen that difficult temperament and atypical development can increase the risk that a child will run into problems. Other personal characteristics can make a boy or girl vulnerable. Once again, I urge you to maintain a balanced view: Be aware of risk factors, but also remember that children are resilient.

DOES YOUR CHILD HAVE A DISABILITY OR ILLNESS?

A youngster might have a physical or intellectual handicap; he might suffer from a chronic illness, such as diabetes, heart or kidney disease, a neurological disorder, or severe allergies. Understandably, parents worry that problems like these might have emotional consequences. Mentally retarded youngsters and those with severe learning disabilities are certainly at greater risk. But my repeated experience is that physically ill or handicapped youngsters show strong resilience, especially if they enjoy good family support.

Consider Aaron and Lee, both ten-year-old diabetic boys. Lee's father died of a diabetes-related heart ailment when the boy was six. His mother, who has not remarried, loves her son and worries about his health, but she also resents all the extra effort his illness demands of her. Lee is a temperamentally anxious, stubborn child, with a low sensory threshold, who has very strong food preferences. His tests, injections, and dietary limitations are a chronic source of conflict with his mother. Lee's reluctance to comply with medical instructions understandably makes his mother very protective—for example, she won't let him go on overnight visits, and she keeps him home from school at the slightest hint of a minor illness. Because he is absent frequently, Lee is behind in most school subjects. He has few friends and is unhappy much of the time. Though many of his problems appear related to the diabetes, they also stem from his difficult temperament and less-than-ideal family situation.

Aaron, on the other hand, is blessed not only with a cheerful personality, but also with well-organized parents who have helped him adapt to the diabetes. His medical care and diet are matters of long-standing routine; he and his parents have found ingenious ways to deal with special events, such as birthday parties. Because they work closely with Aaron's teachers, he has good support in school as well as at home. In contrast to Lee, Aaron is a happy boy, with many friends, who gets along with his family and is successful at school.

HAS YOUR CHILD HAD THIS PROBLEM BEFORE?

Many people have a tendency to develop a particular problem under stress, a phenomenon I call **symptomatic consistency**. One child's unhappiness may be reflected in an upset stomach, while another consistently wets the bed. Or take Matthew: He didn't begin sleeping through the night until after his first birthday; even at age five, he often awakened during the night. Now Matthew is ten and has generally outgrown his sleep problems. But if something is bothering him, disturbed sleep is one of the earliest signs.

IS THERE A MAJOR ISSUE IN YOUR CHILD'S BACKGROUND?

When a youngster has been through a potentially troubling experience—such as divorce, the death of a parent or sibling, or some other traumatic event—parents understandably worry about later repercussions. In some cases, they focus too much and too fearfully on a single issue, blaming it for any and all difficulties.

Serious family issues not only can make youngsters more vulnerable to emotional and behavioral problems, but also may reduce the ability of parents to provide adequate support. In such a situation, it can be helpful to seek assistance from professionals and support groups; you may be able to find relevant books that deal with specific issues at your local library or bookstore.

Certain features of a child's past are associated with specific sensitivities. Here are some examples:

- The death of, or other permanent separation from, a significant person, such as a parent or sibling, can make a child more vulnerable to loss later in life. For example, the youngster who loses a parent at an early age subsequently might have unusually strong reactions to relatively minor separations—a friend moving away, the hospitalization of another family member, or the death of a pet.

- Divorce, especially if it was associated with much conflict and bitterness, can lead to continuing problems with trust and intimacy.

- Frequent moves—whether the entire family or just the child changes residences—are especially stressful for shy children and those who don't readily adapt to change.

- Surviving an accident or disaster can lead to nightmares and troubling vivid memories, even years later. A child who has been through such an experience might startle more easily or be especially cautious and afraid in situations that remind her of what happened.

Once again, I want to emphasize that past events, like any other risk factor, can be countered by the child's resilience and positive elements in her life. Loving parents, good family experiences, personal traits such as being friendly and flexible—all are factors that contribute to a child's strength in the face of adversity.

WHAT ARE YOUR CHILD'S STRENGTHS?

When you're focused on problems, it's easy to overlook your child's positive potential. Shifting gears to think about strengths is helpful in several ways. As I will show you in Part III, a youngster's talents and abilities can be recruited to solve problems. Also, focusing on strengths will make you feel more positive and optimistic.

Start with the characteristics that you admire in your child and the traits that other people compliment. These questions may help you add to your list:

- What are your child's temperamental assets? Does she have a sunny disposition? Is she adaptable? Attentive? Go back over the description you gave earlier to remind yourself of positive characteristics.
- In what areas has your child's development been more rapid than average? Precocity often reflects special talent.
- Is your child creative? Imaginative?
- Does she have artistic abilities? Consider areas like painting, sculpture, drama, writing, and dance.
- Is he healthy? Attractive?
- Does she have athletic talents? Is she graceful? Strong? Well-coordinated?
- Is she intelligent? Does she learn quickly? Is her memory good? Does she have common sense?
- Does he have a good sense of humor?
- Does he have abilities in specific academic areas, such as reading, writing, math, or science?
- Is she a leader?
- Does he have good interpersonal skills? Is he sensitive? Empathetic? Generous?
- Does your child have a good self-image? Is she confident that other people like her? Does she take pride in her work? Is she both positive and realistic in appraising herself?

Here's how I questioned the mother of eight-year-old Jacob. He was a highly active, loud, hot-tempered child; she was a single parent with a demanding career in accounting, worn-out from coping with her son. When I first asked about Jacob's strengths, she needed prompting:

ST: *I can see that he is an attractive, energetic boy.*
MOTHER: *He's energetic, that's for sure.*

ST: I can imagine that he's exhausting at times, but there are positive aspects too. Is he good at sports?

MOTHER: He's a pretty fast runner. The gym teacher told me he's well-coordinated, but he doesn't have the self-control for team sports.

ST: Does he have any talents in the arts?

MOTHER: He's not really artistic. He'll scribble a picture if there's nothing else to do.

ST: I was wondering if he was interested in drama—his voice is so loud and clear.

MOTHER: You can hear him a mile away! As a matter of fact, he does enjoy drama. Whenever there's a play at school, he always wants to be the star.

ST: You might consider theatrical activities outside of school if he is talented.

MOTHER: He'd really like more chances to perform—I'll check into it.

ST: You said his school grades would be good if he behaved better. Is he bright?

MOTHER: Oh yes. He's very smart, in math especially.

ST: What about his interpersonal skills—how is he with other kids?

MOTHER: Better than he is with me, I'll tell you that. He's got lots of friends. Our two little neighbor boys adore him. Their mother is always saying she can't wait until he's old enough to babysit.

ST: It's understandable that when you come home after a long day at work, his wild behavior gets to you. But perhaps you can temper your irritation by remembering that this is a child who is outgoing and well-liked, and who has some good abilities. If you shift your attention to positive areas, and start doing enjoyable things together, you'll derive much more pleasure from him—and he'll see the more positive side of you.

MOTHER: I like the idea of doing something pleasant with him.

ST: Well, you're an accountant, so you're obviously good with *numbers—maybe there's a way to use his talent in math to foster the relationship between you.*

At least as important as the mother's specific ideas is the budding change in her attitude toward Jacob. She is beginning to see the possibility of enjoying good times with her son.

■   ■   ■   ■

This section of the evaluation has looked at your child's normal self. You may have found it painful to think about factors that could make your child's life more difficult. However, understanding vulnerabilities has these important benefits:

- Your attitude will become more sympathetic and accepting.
- Problems can be anticipated. For example, if you know your child has trouble adjusting to new situations, you can prepare him for changes and make transitions easier.
- You can identify areas where extra support is needed and acquire useful expertise. For instance, if your child has a learning disability, you can become familiar with special-education resources.

The next chapter looks at the child's home and school environment.

SEVEN

YOUR CHILD AT HOME AND AT SCHOOL

Parents who are concerned about their child usually wonder if they or someone else is doing something harmful. These questions are typical:

"My mother-in-law says he misbehaves because he's angry that I work full-time. Is that possible?"

"Could he be having toilet accidents, even at age seven, just because of the new baby?"

"My wife and I never argue in front of the kids, but all three of them have been acting out lately. Are they picking up on the tension between the two of us?"

"She's always gotten very good grades before, so the problem must be her new teacher—right?"

This chapter will guide you through a systematic examination of your child's environment. You will be looking at yourselves, your family, and the child's school and peers. Sometimes this uncovers an obvious cause, or **precipitant** for the difficulties. But usually, things are more complex and less certain. Several possible causes might suggest themselves, or there may be no apparent reason for the problems. Even then an examination of the youngster's environment will always reveal opportunities for positive change.

The questions in this chapter cover many more possibilities than are pertinent to any single youngster or family. I suggest you focus on those issues that appear to be significant, and not dwell on matters that seem irrelevant. For some parents, certain areas may be painful to scrutinize. Please remember that the knowledge you gain will be a tool for improving your relationship with your child and your ability to deal with his behavior.

LOOK AT YOURSELF AS A PARENT AND A PERSON

The questions below concern you as a person. I'm not asking you to put yourself under a critical microscope! Certainly it is helpful to be aware of issues that might affect your attitudes and behavior as a parent. But also remember that imperfect people can be excellent parents—provided they make an effort not to impose their own problems on their children.

DESCRIBE YOUR PERSONALITY

In general, an easygoing, well-organized mom or dad has the fewest difficulties. Such a person is likely to be accepting and flexible, yet able to provide the necessary leadership and firmness. Obviously, we can't all be like this—at least not all the time. Most of us have some traits that make parenting more difficult, though we usually can compensate.

When I perform an evaluation, I always ask parents to give me a quick profile of themselves. The questions below are designed to high-light areas that may present problems for you, and perhaps for your child. You and your spouse may be able to offer each other insights. Don't be dismayed if you recognize that aspects of your personality sometimes interfere with parenting. If you know you need to make an extra effort in certain areas, you can take corrective steps.

- *Are you a worrier?* Do you have a tendency to ask anxious "What if?" questions? While proper caution protects a child, undue nervousness can make a youngster anxious.
- *Are you a perfectionist?* Do you set very high standards for yourself? For others? Unless your expectations are realistic, you might be disappointed in your child or subject her to excess pressure.
- *Do you have trouble making up your mind?* Is it hard for you to bring things to a conclusion? A tendency in this direction could make you too prone to negotiate instead of taking a stand. If you're indecisive, you may lose authority with your child.
- *Are you somewhat disorganized?* Do you have trouble sticking to a schedule? If your child needs structure to function well, you would have to make a particular effort to provide it.
- *Do you get angry a lot?* Do you have a tendency to overreact? Extra self-control will be necessary if you happen to have a very sensitive, easily hurt child.
- *Do you go to great lengths to avoid conflict or confrontation?* If you're a peacekeeper, you make a valuable contribution to family serenity, but you might be overly hesitant to impose limits that make your child temporarily unhappy.
- *Is it hard for you to change direction?* Are you sometimes rigid? If your child is a nonconformist, you will need to be more flexible.

WHAT ARE YOUR STRONG POINTS?

Your strengths, like those of your child, can be overlooked when things are going badly. But they are valuable in planning solutions. Think about your interests and about the areas where you feel most competent.

Is there any way you could draw upon the personal assets that make you effective elsewhere? Your patience? Intelligence? Organizing ability? Hobbies and interests?

Here's an example: Like many parents, Karen's mother—director of community relations for a bank—was baffled by the contrast between her success at work and a sense of having failed at home. She was pleased to realize that her professional skills could be tapped to improve her relationship with her nine-year-old daughter.

> ST: *You've said that one of the areas in which you have confrontations with Karen is over chores. You have to nag her; she doesn't do a proper job, and then the two of you wind up arguing.*
>
> MOTHER: *Right. It's a struggle from start to finish.*
>
> ST: *You've also mentioned that you supervise twelve people at work. I assume you're able to give them instructions and require them to meet standards.*
>
> MOTHER: *I hope so! But I can't treat my own daughter like an employee—that would be so cold and impersonal. She's already convinced I don't love her.*
>
> ST: *You're right that you shouldn't treat your daughter as if she were simply a member of your staff. But recruiting your administrative strengths could be a very positive way to deal with Karen. What would you do with an uncooperative secretary?*
>
> MOTHER: *Let's see: I would clarify my expectations by making the job description more explicit, set up more frequent performance reviews, maybe use some incentives to boost motivation. Things like that.*
>
> ST: *There you go! You can use similar techniques with Karen, without in any way sacrificing the caring component of your relationship.*

One idea that Karen's mother borrowed from the office was to send her daughter brief memos, rather than nagging or scolding when there were minor problems with chores. These written reminders were usually effective; more important, they rarely triggered arguments. Because of this and other new approaches, Karen and her mother had fewer confrontations, and their relationship slowly improved.

IS YOUR BACKGROUND INFLUENCING YOUR REACTIONS?

It's only natural to view children through the lens of our own childhood: Our views of parenting are shaped by the parenting we received; our assumptions about children are affected by our own memories. Experience is instructive, but it also can lead us to make assumptions that don't really apply to a particular child.

The questions below are designed to help you gain insight, but I'm not asking you to look for subtleties. It's more productive to focus on areas where there's a clear connection between your background and your relationship with your child.

- *What kind of family do you come from?* Most families are a mixture: generally positive, but with some problems. If your childhood was happy, and your parents were positive models, consider that an asset. However, a troubled family background will *not* automatically make you a bad parent! Being aware of sore points helps you become more conscious of your own behavior in those areas.
- *What were your parents like?* Were they very involved? Strict? Rigid? Loving? Did you feel accepted as a child? How did they discipline you? In general, would you like to be the kind of parent that your parents were, or the very opposite?

Parents sometimes overcompensate for problems they perceive in their own mother or father. I often see parents who feel their own upbringing was excessively strict, and who have gone so far in the other direction that their own children lack adequate structure.

- *Think about other family members: How well did you get along?* Were there any special problems?

A father who had painful experiences with a bullying older brother might overreact to normal quarrels between his own children. A mother whose sister was hospitalized for depression as an adolescent could become unduly alarmed if her eleven-year-old daughter seems sad or dissatisfied.

- *What kind of child were you?* Easy? Difficult? Were you happy? What were your experiences at school? With peers? Does your son or daughter remind you of yourself as a child?

Parents sometimes misperceive a child because they're trying to protect the youngster from some long-ago unhappiness of their own. Here's what Avery's dad told me about his son—and what Avery said about himself:

> FATHER: *It breaks my heart to go to his Little League games. There's my kid warming the bench, just like me at his age. He even looks the same: short and skinny, with glasses. Once in a while he gets to play, and he usually strikes out if he's at bat, or fumbles the ball if the coach puts him in the outfield, and it brings back all those miserable years.*
>
> AVERY: *I'm in Little League, and it's lots of fun. I'm not a good hitter yet, so I don't play much, but I get to sit with the team and high-five my friends. One time I made this awesome catch that won the game.*

- *Do you have children from a previous marriage?* Is your past relationship with them affecting your parenting now? A common example is the man raising a second family who regrets that he wasn't closer to his sons or daughters the first time around. In most cases, this realization is beneficial; however, sometimes such fathers overcompensate.

Dylan's father, who has two children in their twenties from a previous marriage, typifies this pattern. In his relationship with Dylan, age five, he's more like a grandfather than a father—indulgent and easygoing. While it's fine to be a relaxed and openly affectionate parent, Dylan's father has gone too far for this particular child. The boy is impulsive and immature, and he needs a lot of structure. Out of a desire to correct his own earlier parenting deficiencies, the father is undermining his wife's efforts to provide necessary limits for Dylan.

WHAT KIND OF EXAMPLE DO YOU SET?

Most mothers and fathers are very much aware of teaching children standards and values. But they may be less conscious of how much youngsters pick up from adult behavior. Even intelligent and perceptive parents have blind spots in this regard: Their child is a chip off the old block, but they don't see it. In effect, they're sending a double message with actions that contradict their instructions.

Carlos and his family came to me at the suggestion of his second-grade teacher. I brought the parents into my office to talk while the boy played in my waiting room. Carlos is too forceful and belligerent, they told me; he yells at other children and pushes them around when he doesn't get his way. Their voices rose as they described a recent incident. Carlos heard them and opened the door. "Hey, Carlos!" his father said with an angry gesture. "You're supposed to stay out there." His mother added, "Turn around and march!" Obvious as it seems from this description, these parents did not see the connection between their child's behavior and their own aggressive style.

A more subtle example: Alice, age twelve, had a long history of discipline problems in school. "The teachers are dumb," she told me. "They don't know what they're doing." According to Alice, school rules should be accepted by students only if they make sense.

When I asked Alice's parents about themselves, I learned that they had strong antiestablishment values. Her mother, a social worker at an agency for the homeless, described how she had lived in a radical commune in the 1960s and proudly said that she has kept the faith. Alice's father, who develops educational software for a major publishing firm, spoke with contempt about the company's willingness to sacrifice quality for the sake of profits. Alice had joined her parents at political demonstrations from the time she was a baby, with placards tied to her stroller.

Because of her background, Alice was much more aware of social issues than most youngsters her age; she had a sincere desire to help the underprivileged and did volunteer work with the children of homeless families in her mother's agency. Her parents were proud that their influence had led her in this direction. But they didn't see the connection between their own willingness to challenge authority and Alice's attitude toward her teachers. In family sessions, I helped them teach her the lesson they've learned: to maintain their ideals and individuality without pointless rebellion.

DO YOU HAVE SERIOUS PERSONAL PROBLEMS?

All of us occasionally have personal difficulties or find ourselves under pressure. Few mothers or fathers can accurately claim that their children have never seen the fallout. Indeed, one of the first things parents worry about at troubled times is the possible impact on their child. In answering the questions below, limit yourself to problems that are serious or chronic:

- Do you suffer from a mental illness, or are you addicted to drugs or alcohol?
- Do you have a significant physical illness?
- Has there been a major upheaval in your personal life, such as a divorce or the death of someone you loved?
- Are you having serious financial difficulties? Is there any unusual pressure at work?
- Do your parents or other loved ones have major problems that affect you?

Perhaps the best way to determine if your parenting is affected by your problems is to look at the child. Consider these possible signs:

- The child directly expresses distress. Suppose a single father has been talking about layoffs at work. If his eight-year-old daughter is too exposed to his anxiety, she might begin to have nightmares and to ask worried questions like, "Will we become homeless if you lose your job?"
- The child is bewildered or fearful. For example, if his mother drinks too much, he avoids her, or cries and says he's afraid of her.
- Other people tell you that the child is affected. I sometimes repeat to the parents what their child has told me. Hearing statements like these always motivates parents to make an extra effort to protect their children from adult issues:

"My parents are always fighting."

"When my daddy gets angry, he acts like a scary monster."

"I can't tell my mom about my problem because it would make her even more depressed."

Even if you have quite severe problems, you can partially insulate your child from the troubled parts of your life. I'm not suggesting you pretend that nothing is wrong—as you saw in Chapter 4, I believe in open communication with a child. But you can filter information in a way that protects the youngster without dishonesty.

If possible, it's best to tell children about your problems during a planned discussion, rather than at a time when you feel upset and overwhelmed. Sometimes parents, in an effort to reassure a child, deny there's a problem. But since the youngster can plainly see that something is wrong, denial makes for more insecurity, not less. It's far better to validate the child's perceptions and to offer a developmentally appropriate explanation. For example, the single father might tell his eight-year-old girl, "I might be laid off at work, so I'm starting to look at other jobs, just in case." But his daughter doesn't need to know how anxious he feels about an upcoming interview—that's an adult issue.

ARE THERE FAMILY DIFFICULTIES?

A strong, harmonious family is a wonderful source of support for a youngster. But if your family, like so many, falls short of this ideal, you may worry about the negative impact on your child.

The questions below cover some, but by no means all, of the family issues that may be relevant to a youngster's problems. So feel free to expand the list to include changes like a remarriage or having an elderly relative join your household. Be especially aware of anything that occurred around the time you first noticed the difficulties.

As you think about your family, try to focus on opportunities for positive change. You may be able to resolve the difficulties, or at least insulate the child from them; family members may have compensatory strengths. And always remember that children are resilient. Most youngsters can be happy and function well despite less-than-ideal circumstances.

Is Your Marriage a Problem for Your Child?

While a loving, respectful marriage is the best relationship between a mother and father, children can thrive in other situations. Of course, some family configurations, such as blended stepfamilies, require greater adaptation. But you should not assume that your child will have problems simply because a situation calls for him to adjust.

Parents sometimes are needlessly upset if a child overhears them quarreling; their concern may be exacerbated if the youngster expresses distress—for example, if she yells, "Stop making all that noise!" However, occasional arguments, in the context of a generally good marriage, are not a serious problem for children. What creates difficulty is long-standing, recurrent conflict and open hostility between spouses.

Marital discord is more harmful if antagonistic parents inappropriately involve their child. Sometimes a mother or father attempts to make an ally of the youngster: One parent may criticize the other in front of him, use him to send negative messages, or undermine his relationship with the other parent. Or an unhappy mom or dad might look to a son or daughter for the companionship missing in the marriage.

If you and your spouse are having problems, consider honestly if you're involving the child in your conflicts. Ask yourself if you see an impact on the youngster. Here are some signs:

- He becomes scared or upset during fights, or begs you to stop.
- She asks questions like, "Are you getting a divorce?" "Are you going to leave Mommy?" "Do you still love Daddy?"
- A more subtle reaction is for the child to become a **lightning rod:** She behaves badly in a subconscious effort to deflect the family problems onto herself.

Rita's parents consulted me because their daughter had become intolerably fresh and defiant. She responded to her mother's requests with, "You can't tell me what to do!" When her father scolded her, she told him, "Oh, shut up, you dummy." She missed few opportunities to provoke them.

This couple agreed on little other than their assessment of Rita. Their marriage was chronically unsatisfactory, but it had hit a low point shortly before her troubling behavior started. I told them, "In a sense, your daughter is acting generously: She's drawing your anger towards herself, so you won't direct it against each other. Unless you resolve your marital difficulties—or at least protect Rita from them—she may increasingly feel that she is responsible for your problems."

ARE YOU IN THE MIDST OF A DIVORCE?

Ending a marriage is always very difficult. But sometimes it's even more damaging to maintain a nonviable relationship. If you've reached that point and are separating or divorcing, good parenting will pose an extra challenge. Feelings will be volatile. Even if you and your ex-spouse want very much to protect your children, it's almost impossible to avoid occasional mistakes. You may argue in front of them, even though you agreed not to; you may make critical comments about the other parent that you later regret. Try to hold such behavior to a minimum, no matter how bitter your feelings are about your ex-spouse. Always remember that a child is entitled to a relationship with both parents.

The same guidelines I offered for discussing other adult problems with children also apply to divorce. It's best to tell the child about the end of your marriage in a planned discussion, so that the atmosphere is relatively calm. You can acknowledge problems without offering inappropriate details about adult issues, such as infidelity.

IS YOUR CHILD AFFECTED BY A SIBLING?

Brothers and sisters can contribute to a child's problems. A chronically demanding sibling—such as one who is disturbed, handicapped, or very difficult—can affect a youngster directly. In addition, such a sibling significantly drains his parents' energy and thus deprives his brothers and sisters of their fair share of attention.

A related pattern, which I often see in families with a difficult child, is that the "easy" sibling becomes a goody-two-shoes: an overly obedient, conforming youngster who never makes trouble. This is not the same as being a kind, empathetic child who tries to help. The personality of the "too-good" child is founded on pleasing others rather than paying attention to his own needs. Such a person can run into trouble later in life.

Children with "star" siblings often suffer from comparison. For instance, an average student could come to feel deficient if his teachers and parents constantly remind him about the stellar academic performance of his exceptionally talented older brother.

Less commonly, a youngster may have problems as the direct result of a sibling. This could happen if the brother or sister is aggressive or exhibits bizarre behavior. Here are signs you might notice in your child:

- She's afraid of her brother or avoids him. It's normal for an older child to avoid the younger one, but not vice versa.
- She constantly tries to please her sister and caters to her in a way that seems inappropriate.
- He is very worried about his brother.

IS SIBLING RIVALRY A CONCERN?

Many parents overemphasize the significance of quarrels and jealousy between brothers and sisters. This exaggeration can reflect issues in their own lives. A mother who is unhappy about her relationship with an estranged sister may overreact to minor disagreements between her daughters. Or parents may have unrealistic expectations, like the newly married mother and father in a blended family who assume that real stepsiblings get along as well as the fictional Brady Bunch.

Keep in mind that children express anger and hostility more openly than adults do, and that they get over these often superficial feelings much more quickly. If your children fight, but also enjoy each other, you probably have little cause for concern. Obviously, frequent arguments can create an unpleasant family atmosphere, even if they aren't actually damaging.

When hostility between siblings is more extreme, family issues are almost always involved. Here are some questions to ask yourself:

- Might you and your spouse be setting a negative example by your own confrontational, argumentative style? Sometimes parents do a great deal of fighting in front of their children, then are surprised that the youngsters fight with each other.

- Do you place excessive emphasis on fairness and family togetherness? Parents may unwittingly perpetuate sibling rivalry by setting unrealistically high standards for equity. If you buy a present for one child, you do *not* have to automatically get one for her brother. Nor is it reasonable to insist on constant harmony and affection between siblings.

- Do you feel obliged to settle all arguments between your children? If you interfere too quickly, you may actually fuel the problem. The youngsters will become dependent upon you to resolve minor differences, instead of learning to get along by themselves.

ARE OTHER FAMILY MEMBERS INVOLVED?

In some households, parents aren't the only adults who contribute significantly to the youngster's upbringing. Other people may have strong emotional ties to the child, spend a lot of time with him, or exercise authority over him. Or they could have an indirect impact on the youngster because they affect you. Such individuals include a divorced parent who doesn't live with the child, a stepparent, a grandparent, or a housekeeper.

Children's lives are enriched by good relationships with adults other than their parents. Your son's happy visits with a devoted grandfather may compensate for tensions elsewhere in his life. His stepmother may be a resource during a troubled period, because she knows him well but can be more objective than you or his father.

On the other hand, children may be adversely affected by other adults. A caretaker might be overindulgent—or overly critical; a non-custodial parent may be inconsistent about expectations. In an extreme case, there could even be emotional or physical abuse. Here are some signs of problems:

- Your child complains about the other individual, and doesn't want to be with him.
- The person criticizes your child, and says she's having trouble coping with his behavior.
- You feel uneasy about this person.

Youngsters also suffer if conflicts arise between parents and other important people in their lives. A parent might become jealous of a housekeeper's relatively untroubled relationship with a child; a stepfather could feel undermined in the area of discipline by an overly indulgent mother. Two signs that hostility between you and another adult might be contributing to your child's difficulties:

- The child has problems making transitions between the two of you.
- The youngster plays you off against each other.

This mother thought that her mother-in-law was a factor in the rude, demanding behavior of her seven-year-old son, Gavin:

ST: *Tell me about her relationship with Gavin.*

MOTHER: *She takes care of him after school—we're saving for a house. She lets him walk all over her, so he thinks she's the greatest, and I'm his mean old Mom.*

ST: *How do you get along with your mother-in-law?*

MOTHER: *Not very well. We're so different. My career is very important to me; she's a Betty Crocker type straight from the 1950s. She thinks it's practically child abuse for a woman to work before her kids are in college. So there are always the little snide remarks.*

ST: *Does she make these comments in front of Gavin?*

MOTHER: *Oh yes. The other day it was, "We played Chinese checkers this afternoon and Gavin had so much fun. Maybe you could play with him someday when you're not so busy." She acts like I never spend any time with him, which is untrue.*

ST: *It sounds as if she is too competitive with you. But you need to look at your own participation in this. If you're sure Gavin is being adversely affected by the overt tension between the two of you, it has to stop. The ideal would be to work out your problems. But if you can't, you might decide to limit your mother-in-law's involvement, despite its convenience. And certainly give more attention to improving your relationship with Gavin.*

A common source of difficulty for the child of divorced parents is their continuing antagonism toward each other. Ryan's father asked me to meet with him, his ex-wife, and their ten-year-old son, because the boy refused to visit him. He assumed that his ex-wife had encouraged Ryan's animosity. The couple had divorced eighteen months earlier, at the mother's insistence, despite the father's reluctance to end the marriage.

At the time I saw them, the mother was not obviously hostile toward her ex-husband. However, she was overly sympathetic when Ryan complained about his father. This was part of the problem, but the main difficulty was that the father had confused and upset Ryan by treating him more as an adult friend than as a son: He confided in the boy about his loneliness and insecurities; he asked Ryan for advice on how to reestablish the relationship with his ex-wife. He also demanded too much attention. If the boy asked to end a visit a few hours early so he could attend a birthday party or some other special event with his friends, his father chastised him for being "unloving and ungrateful."

I suggested that both parents stop discussing each other with their son, and they agreed to do so. Most of all, Ryan and his father needed to establish a more appropriate relationship. They began discussing interests and activities they could share. In several private sessions with the father, I explained the importance of maintaining a distinction between the issues of adults and children; I also helped him understand that his son was not rejecting him when he occasionally asked to do something with his friends. During our meetings, the father's unresolved feelings about his ex-wife and the divorce became evident. With my encouragement, he decided to resume therapy with a psychologist who had been helpful to him before his divorce.

I find that divorced parents usually are able to settle disputes and negotiate compromises based on what's best for the child—provided each has achieved closure, a full acceptance that their marriage is truly ended. This may take time. But once the powerful and often irrational emotions are behind them, and their feelings are no longer raw and hurt, ex-spouses usually can function cooperatively and make decisions about their child without anger or vindictiveness.

IS SCHOOL AN ISSUE?

If your child isn't having problems at school, don't spend much time on this section of the evaluation. Just glance over the questions to see if they suggest any useful ideas. For instance, if he's thriving in a highly structured kindergarten, you might think of ways to add structure at home. You can adapt the questions below to any other places where your child has difficulty, such as camp, child care, or activity groups.

School can be relevant to a child's problems in two ways: as cause or as setting. Stresses at school can produce emotional problems outside school as well. Examples would be the seven-year-old boy who becomes anxious because he has an overly critical teacher, or the nine-year-old girl whose self-image deteriorates because she can't keep up with her classmates.

On the other hand, the fact that the child has problems during the school day doesn't necessarily mean that school is the source. It may merely be the setting for expression of difficulties that originate in the home or elsewhere. For example, an eight-year-old boy might be upset because his mother has been very ill. As a result, he forgets to do homework assignments and daydreams in class.

Understanding why a child has problems at school—and determining whether school is cause or setting—will take you a long way toward finding a solution. If you aren't sure, ask yourself these questions:

- *Is your child having similar problems anywhere else?* If not, that points to school as an important factor.

- *Does he have these problems when school isn't in session?* A "yes" suggests that the difficulties don't originate with the school.
- *Did the problems begin when something changed at school*—for example, at the start of a new semester, a new class, or a disruption such as a long teacher absence?
- *Does the teacher believe that the school is causing the difficulty?* Don't hesitate to ask: A good teacher will be honest about deficiencies in the school environment and will report on problems objectively.
- *Are other children having similar reactions?* This question was illuminating for Leila's parents. Their daughter, who had breezed through preschool and kindergarten, disliked first grade. She began dawdling in the mornings and developed weekdays-only stomachaches. When Leila's mother checked around, she discovered that several other children seemed distressed. It turned out that Leila's teacher was new and inexperienced and had trouble controlling the class. She yelled a lot and resorted to punishment too often.

Chapter 11 discusses school problems—including school refusal, hyperactivity, and learning difficulties—and suggests ways for parents to collaborate with teachers on the youngster's behalf. Such a collaboration, and the extra support a child can get from a compassionate teacher, are always helpful whether or not school is causing the problems.

ARE PEER RELATIONSHIPS A FACTOR?

I always take it as a good sign when parents tell me that their child is well-liked by other youngsters and has a circle of nice friends. When this is not the case, and parents are concerned about a child's relations with peers, the issues can be difficult to sort out.

Peer problems often happen when you're not around, and some youngsters are reluctant to discuss them with parents. So you may have incomplete or inaccurate information about the situation. Also, your own childhood experiences, and the natural tendency to be on your child's side, can distort your view.

A misperception I see frequently involves the parent who is worried that a child doesn't have enough friends—but when I talk to the youngster, I find that the issue is one of preference. Some children like to have just one or two close friends, instead of being part of a larger group. Also, a normally shy child will form new friendships more slowly than an outgoing youngster. When a youngster is happy, generally functioning well, and following his usual friendship pattern, there's no reason to worry.

If your child complains about other children's treatment of him, have a planned discussion to get a clearer picture of the problem. Ask questions: Is he being bullied? Teased? Excluded? Pressured to misbehave? Indicate your willingness to listen and sympathize, but curb the natural impulse to respond immediately with instructive comments such as, "Why don't you just walk away if she's mean?" or "And what did *you* do to provoke him?"

Children don't always confide in their parents when they have problems with peers. Therefore, you also should be alert to obvious changes in mood or behavior: Is he avoiding any child or group of children? Does he suddenly refuse to go to the playground? Does he seem frightened?

As is true of school, peers can cause difficulties—or peer relations may be a setting for problems that originate elsewhere. When your child is having trouble with other children, it's only natural for you to assume the fault lies with them, especially if the difficulty is teasing or bullying.

Some questions to help you tell the difference:

- *Does your child have a pattern of similar trouble in more than one setting:* at school this year, in previous grades, in the neighborhood, or at camp? If the problems seem confined to one place, the cause is most likely poor fit. For example, a studious child might have trouble making friends in an athletically oriented school.

- *Are other children suffering the same way?* If so, it's possible that an antisocial group or individual is responsible for the trouble. Are there cliques at your child's school? Preteens are notorious for their shifting alliances, which often result in one child being temporarily excluded or rejected by former friends.

Difficult as it is for parents to accept, the youngster who is chronically excluded, teased, or bullied usually is contributing to this response by her own behavior. Children with impaired self-image frequently run into trouble with peers. Such a youngster may become a braggart or a bully, as well as a victim. She could avoid contact with other children or gravitate toward troublemakers. Peer relationships are likely to improve when other changes are made in her life, and her self-image gets better.

■   ■   ■   ■

You have now completed the parental evaluation—a detailed examination of the problems, your child, and his environment. This thorough look should have given you a greater understanding of the situation. Even more important, I hope that the evaluation has helped you begin a fundamental attitudinal shift: If you're now able to view your child, his problems, and your family more objectively and sympathetically, you've already accomplished a great deal.

Performing the evaluation has given you an opportunity to practice new communication techniques—especially the planned discussion— with your spouse and child. By now you should be able to talk about sensitive issues more calmly and constructively than in the past.

Perhaps the evaluation helped you recognize that the situation is more serious than you had realized: the symptoms are multiple, chronic, or disruptive; or maybe there are other major family difficulties. In that case, professional assistance is needed—something I will discuss further in Chapter 12.

I want to underscore the fact that parents can *always* provide some help to a child with problems. This is true even if they aren't certain what caused the difficulties and even if they determine that professional assistance is required.

Going through the parental evaluation probably has suggested many specific ways to improve your child's situation. Part III offers numerous additional ideas.

PART III

ADULT
LEADERSHIP

EIGHT

ACTIVE ACCEPTANCE AND YOUR CHILD'S SELF-IMAGE

If there's a single key to emotional well-being, it is self-acceptance: a realistic understanding of who we are, both our human flaws and our positive attributes. This benign self-appreciation is the foundation of self-esteem. It allows us to care about others as well as ourselves and permits us to receive love without losing independence. Accepting oneself is not at all the same as self-centeredness. Rather, it's a sense of being worthy, though not perfect—remember the word "realistic."

You can foster this all-important feeling in your child by accepting him. Acceptance is one of the most precious gifts you can offer: letting your child know that you enjoy him and are proud of him and that he brings you pleasure simply because of who he is. Acceptance is grounded in understanding as well as in positive feelings. It means having appropriate expectations and acknowledging your child as a separate, unique individual who may be quite different from you and from your concept of how a child should be.

Much as we love our children, we don't always accept them. Rarely do well-meaning parents go to the extreme of overt rejection. But they may express lack of acceptance in other ways: by their disappointment, frequent criticism, overly demanding expectations—and even by excessive indulgence that reflects their low expectations.

Acceptance may not be easy when a child has problems. Understandably, parents feel disappointed. They may compare him to other youngsters and find themselves envying mothers and fathers whose children seem happier, better behaved, more popular, or more successful at school; they may become angry, irritated, or critical. Battle-weary parents sometimes interpret a youngster's behavior in a consistently negative way: They think he's being mean or deliberately misbehaving just to annoy them. Having such feelings about a child is very painful for parents. They feel demoralized, trapped, and guilty.

Children facing chronic nonacceptance tend to have two reactions: They internalize their parents' unfavorable assessment, or they fight it— and sometimes they do both. Either response triggers negative patterns within the family. When a self-critical youngster becomes sad or depressed and gives up trying, that leads to further failure and more negative reactions. If the youngster rebels, nonacceptance results in family conflict, which creates its own emotional distress.

I believe that the natural impulse of parents is to accept their child. If they don't, it's usually not because they're unloving, but because their expectations don't fit the youngster's nature and capacities. Once parents understand their child and see him or her more clearly, acceptance usually follows automatically. As you will see, a different attitude, along with new ways of treating your child, can dramatically reverse many negative patterns.

I use the term **active acceptance** to describe the *choice* parents can make to look at their child objectively but positively. This is not at all the same as bitterly resigning yourself to disappointment or swallowing feelings of anger. Active acceptance is an attitude based on understanding.

Once you have a clearer sense of who your child is, your expectations become more realistic, and you begin to appreciate his strengths. Instead of feeling thwarted and anticipating failure, you develop a sense of optimism. Parents are greatly relieved when they experience this transformation. Often a mother or father tells me, "I have renewed faith in my child and in myself as a parent."

If things have been going very badly with your child, active acceptance may seem impossible. Parents in this situation sometimes ask me such questions as "What's there to like about him?" and "How can I force myself to accept her?" Adopting a new attitude may seem like an uphill struggle. Instead, try to think of it as taking a new route. Once you're on a different path, moving in the right direction will become much easier.

This chapter offers specific suggestions to help you accept your child. In part, active acceptance is something that takes place in your mind and enables you to look at the youngster with new eyes. A more accepting attitude will produce many subtle changes in your behavior. In addition, you can consciously adopt new approaches.

FOCUS ON YOUR CHILD'S ASSETS

When a youngster has problems, her strong points may be overlooked. Remind yourself of your child's evident strengths—the ones you listed in the parental evaluation—and actively seek other positive characteristics.

LOOK FOR SUBTLE TALENTS

Some positive attributes are more visible than others. If your child is articulate, you're probably aware of it, but perhaps you haven't noticed that she's a good listener. You might take for granted the personality traits that make your child easy to get along with. Or maybe you discount her talents in an area you don't value. Adopting a broader view of strengths will give you a more positive attitude.

This kind of change was a key ingredient in the case of Dikembe, age nine. His parents consulted me on the advice of his teacher after a conference at which they discovered that the boy had lied about his poor school grades: He told his parents that he had lost his report card, but that his marks were very good. To explain why his parents hadn't signed the report card, Dikembe told the teacher that they were vacationing in Africa. Suspicious of this tale, the teacher called his house, and the lie unraveled. There were additional concerns: Though Dikembe appeared happy at school, he seemed sad and withdrawn at home; his parents described his relationship with his father as "very tense."

Dikembe's dad was a self-made man who had worked his way out of poverty and was now a top executive at a major department store chain. Academic talent and leadership ability had been the keys to his success. Dikembe had no similar gifts: His intelligence was about average, and he was content to be a follower. His father, who was seen as a role model for boys in his community, tried hard to encourage his son to follow in his footsteps: He pressed Dikembe to run for class president and offered to help him make posters; he worked closely with his son on homework and school projects and constantly exhorted him to make the extra effort to excel. The father not only was personally disappointed and puzzled by Dikembe's "lack of ambition," as he put it; he also feared that his son would see himself as a failure if he couldn't live up to his father's achievements.

I urged him to recognize that leaders and geniuses are not the only people valued by others. Dikembe was friendly, good-humored, and supportive. Other children, including the class leaders, looked to him for companionship and encouragement. Once his father began thinking in this direction, he realized his son had many of the positive traits he admired in successful adults.

The father's new attitude toward Dikembe manifested itself in many subtle changes. He continued to supervise the boy's homework, but there was less emphasis on grades. When his son told him about a friend's accomplishment, he shared the enthusiasm instead of saying, "Why couldn't you do that?" Though my treatment of Dikembe dealt with other issues too, his father's acceptance was an essential part of the solution.

THINK ABOUT THE BROADER PICTURE

Parents who are too focused on a child's limitations can be encouraged by considering the positive aspects of negative characteristics. Easily upset children often are unusually sensitive to the feelings of others, because their own emotions are so acute. A cautious, inhibited youngster, who holds back from beneficial experiences, will also avoid foolish risks. Stubbornness and defiance, which can be so annoying to parents, are linked to more positive persistence and independent thinking.

When parents adopt an accepting attitude, they can acknowledge negative traits without feeling overwhelmed by them. I'm always gratified to see a more benevolent attitude emerging when I work with the parents of an unusually difficult youngster. When I tell them, "This is no cookie-cutter child; she's one of a kind!" and they can laugh wryly but appreciatively, I know that acceptance has begun.

LOOK TO THE FUTURE

The very traits that are so upsetting now might benefit your child later on. For instance, persistently irregular sleeping and eating patterns, though inconvenient for parents, can be useful in careers that demand flexible hours. A high energy level, if appropriately channeled, is an asset in sales and other occupations. An intense, dramatic personality augurs well for a career in the performing arts.

KEEP YOUR OWN ISSUES SEPARATE

Acceptance requires not only that you have a positive attitude, but also that you recognize the child as a separate person. Sometimes clear vision is clouded by our own issues, so we make assumptions that aren't based on who the child truly is.

When parents describe their children's thoughts or emotions, I always ask, "How do you know?" Often they can point to specific things the youngster said or did. But sometimes they're jumping to conclusions:

"Anyone would feel bad if they didn't get into the top reading group."

"All the child-rearing books say that older siblings are jealous of the new baby."

"I remember how frustrated and angry I used to get when I was teased."

When parents make unwarranted assumptions, I remind them, "We're talking about your daughter, not about you as a child or about some theoretical youngster." Here are some questions to help you decide if your own problems and assumptions are interfering with a clear perception of your child:

ARE YOU MAGNIFYING THE SITUATION?

Unresolved personal issues can cause us to see a child's behavior in an exaggerated way: Something in the situation or in the youngster reminds us of a struggle we've been through or a conflicted relationship from the past, so we give the problem weighted and fearful significance. I call this the magnifying-glass effect.

If you have a strong reaction to a child's problem—especially if it seems out of proportion—ask yourself: Why am I reacting so strongly? Might my child feel differently about this? Are her motives the same as mine would be? Recognizing the reason for your exaggerated response goes a long way toward reducing it.

A magnifying-glass issue was one factor in the troubled relationship between Christa, age eleven, and her mother. The girl and her parents came to me after Christa threatened to run away. She was a moody child; her mother was anxious and overinvolved. If Christa was visiting a friend, she was expected to "check in" every few hours. When she called, her mother would question her: "How are you feeling? Is everything okay?" Sometimes Christa welcomed this solicitude, but more often she exploded with, "Stop bugging me! Get off my back!" and slammed down the phone.

When I questioned the mother about her own background, I learned that her older sister had been an unhappy, rebellious teenager who attempted suicide. This caused the mother to exaggerate the significance of her daughter's moods and worry excessively about them. Simply making that connection helped the mother understand that she was magnifying her daughter's moodiness. As she became less fearful, she was able to give Christa more freedom; this reduced a significant area of conflict between them, and their relationship improved.

DO YOU IDENTIFY TOO STRONGLY WITH YOUR CHILD?

We all identify closely with those we love: We're lifted by their joys and hurt by their suffering. But sometimes this closeness makes us forget that the other person is a separate, autonomous individual. That's more likely to happen with a child than with other adults, especially when the youngster resembles us in physical appearance and personality.

Here are some signs of overidentification:

- You believe you usually know what your child is thinking or feeling. A caring, observant parent often can make excellent guesses. But acceptance requires that you be open to surprises.
- The youngster disputes your perceptions and assumptions. She might say things like, "You think you can read my mind, but you can't!"

or "I don't care if *you* always wanted to go to overnight camp—*I* don't want to."

- You use the word *we* when you really mean the child. For example, if someone asks you where he goes to school, you say, "We're at Westwood Elementary."

DOES YOUR CHILD REMIND YOU OF SOMEONE ELSE?

You may misperceive your child because he resembles another person you know. An example is Alan, age nine. His mother, who recently had gone through a bitter divorce, described her life with Alan as "guerrilla warfare." She felt that he misbehaved and annoyed her deliberately to punish her for the divorce. Now Alan was asking to live with his father. Despite their struggles, she loved her son and didn't want him to leave; moreover, her ex-husband was unenthusiastic about accepting full-time responsibility for the boy. She came to me in the hope of improving her relationship with Alan.

At our first meeting, the mother spent almost twenty minutes detailing the similarities between Alan and his dad: There was a strong physical resemblance; both were picky eaters, with similar food prejudices; they even had the same habit of twirling a lock of hair while watching television. Whenever Alan's mother looked at her son, she saw his father, so that minor transgressions were magnified by hostile interpretations. Finally I said to her, "You've told me all the ways in which Alan is like your ex-husband. Now tell me how he is *not* like him."

To her credit, Alan's mother immediately grasped my point. In subsequent meetings, as she began to understand the role that her own issues were playing in her perceptions of her son, she found she was far less irritable with him. She was able to ignore minor comments and actions that previously would have triggered an angry response. In subsequent weeks, she and Alan built upon this initial improvement. Four months later, at a follow-up visit, she reported that their relationship was better, and that Alan no longer asked to live with his father.

DO YOU EXPECT YOUR CHILD TO PLAY A ROLE?

Sometimes a youngster gets typecast. Parents may then misperceive his behavior because it's colored by the role they expect him to perform. Generally, an honest recognition of the situation suffices: When parents realize what's happening, they take steps to change. If the pattern is entrenched, and despite their best efforts they find themselves slipping back into familiar patterns, professional help is needed.

Here are some common inappropriate roles for children:

- *The "best friend."* A situation I regularly see in my practice involves a parent—it could be a mother or father, married or single—who lacks fulfilling adult relationships and turns to the child for companionship. If the parents have marital problems, the child may have been pressed into the role of confidant or even surrogate spouse.

Lydia, age ten, was described by her mother as "more like a sister than a daughter." The mother was very shy and had few adult friends; though her marriage was free of conflict, her husband spent most of his spare time on home-improvement projects and had little interest in going out. As she grew up, Lydia became her mom's companion and escort. Gradually, a pattern developed in which the mother didn't go to a movie, shop for clothes, or visit relatives unless Lydia joined her. They spent most weekends together.

Because the mother saw Lydia as a friend instead of as her child, she felt rejected whenever the girl decided to spend a weekend afternoon with a group of classmates, rather than going on a mother-daughter excursion. Lydia was ambivalent: At times she enjoyed being treated as a grown-up; but she felt angry and guilty when her mother's demands kept her from being with her friends. After she developed headaches that her pediatrician suspected were stress-related, the doctor referred her to me.

Lydia's mother was upset by the idea that her relationship with her daughter might be causing the girl's headaches. "But we're so close!" she protested. I explained that closeness is not the only measure of a healthy adult-child relationship. Lydia did not need treatment;

however, I suggested the mother think about the reasons she hadn't developed meaningful adult relationships and consider if she might benefit from therapy.

- *The perfect sibling.* When I address parent groups on the subject of temperamentally difficult children, I am often asked if these youngsters tend to have emotional problems when they reach adulthood. The answer surprises my audiences: More of my adult patients had difficult brothers or sisters than were difficult children themselves.

When a family has one child with special problems—such as a difficult child, or one who is handicapped or chronically ill—brothers or sisters may be recruited into the role of the perfect child. Such youngsters are overpraised for their good behavior. They learn not to make trouble and to please others rather than asserting their own needs. This can leave them vulnerable to emotional problems.

If you're overburdened by the demands of one child, it's understandable that you might expect your other children to help. This is not a problem, provided the demands are not excessive. Pay attention, however, if a child is overly compliant, sweet, and uncomplaining.

- *The spokesperson.* Children sometimes are tacitly encouraged to express sentiments that the parent is unwilling to voice. A common example is the boy or girl who is used as a pawn in marital conflict. That happened with Nina, age six. A disagreeable pattern developed when her father returned home from work. Nina would say, "Go away! I want to be with Mommy." The father would become hurt and respond angrily; Nina would burst into tears. Her mother would then rush to comfort her daughter, and the father would withdraw to his den. Nina was afraid of her father, but she also loved him and wanted his approval. With her mom, she was clingy and demanding.

The parents, though outwardly polite to each other, had a troubled relationship and were seeing a marriage counselor. In a private session with the mother, I pointed out that she was making Nina her spokesperson by allowing her to be rude to her father. Once she realized that this was inappropriate, and that Nina needed a strong, loving relationship with her dad, she resolved to take a firm stand. Nina's behavior toward her father improved as a result.

ADJUST YOUR EXPECTATIONS

Realistic expectations are grounded in an understanding of your child's true self and take account of his innate nature, abilities, and developmental level. When parents don't see the youngster clearly, their expectations may be inappropriate, and the child may be unable to meet them. When parents recognize that their expectations need adjustment and that the youngster isn't disappointing them on purpose, the stage is set for a more positive attitude.

I'm very much concerned that some parents and teachers seem to regard an average child as unacceptable. One result is what I call the **pressured prince or princess:** a youngster who is materially indulged and also subjected to exceedingly high expectations.

Adam, age nine, attended a highly competitive private school that normally admitted students on the basis of aptitude tests. Though Adam's scores had been clearly below the cutoff, his parents—both prominent business executives—got him into the school through their connections.

Adam fell behind almost immediately. His parents arranged for extensive testing for subtle learning disabilities; none were found. With considerable help from private tutors, he managed to complete the first three grades. But by the middle of fourth grade, his schoolwork had sharply deteriorated. He had few friends, in part because he was boastful and sometimes bullied other children. After many conferences and efforts to improve the situation, the headmaster finally told Adam's mother and father to find another school for him. They called me to request an evaluation, hoping that I could change the headmaster's mind.

School problems were the chief concern of Adam's parents, but there were other worrisome difficulties. Adam had a facial tic; he seemed anxious and sad, and often made self-critical comments like, "I'm the class dummy" and "No one wants to play with me." His mom and dad tried to boost his morale by complimenting him frequently and telling him how much they loved him. They gave him lavish electronic toys, partly to cheer him up and partly to help him attract friends. Instead of having the desired effect, their extravagance was making him materialistic and demanding.

Adam's parents were startled when I told them I agreed with the headmaster's assessment and thought they should find a less academically rigorous school for their son.

FATHER: *But this is a first-rate school. We want him to have the best.*

ST: *There's a difference between helping your child be the best he can be and pushing him to be something he isn't.*

MOTHER: *I know he could do better if he tried harder. If we could only figure out how to motivate him, so he would put more effort into his work, I'm sure his grades would improve a lot.*

ST: *Yes, it's true that he could do better than he's been doing. But that doesn't change the reality of the situation, which is that the work is too hard for him.*

FATHER: *You're telling us to lower our aspirations for Adam. Well, I refuse to do that.*

ST: *It's perfectly okay to expect things of your child, to have hopes and dreams. But your vision must be based on an appreciation of who Adam truly is.*

FATHER: *If you can't help us, we'll find someone else. We've got to—it just kills me to think how he'd feel about leaving his school.*

MOTHER: *I'm so disappointed.* (She began to cry.)

ST: *Are you disappointed for Adam or for yourself?*

MOTHER: *Both. I know he's going to be very upset. But I admit that I'm disappointed for myself too.*

ST: *What exactly disappoints you?*

MOTHER: *Look, I grew up in a small town and went to a crummy public school with a run-down building and huge classes, because my parents couldn't afford private school. I was proud that we could do so much better for Adam, that he could have chances I didn't have.*

FATHER: *Of course we're disappointed. Our son has to leave a top-notch school and go someplace second-rate. This will limit his prep-school options, which affects the kind of college he gets into—and his whole life, if you think about it.*

ST: *You have to ask yourself what you really want for your son. Adam's self-esteem has suffered because he's in a school where he can't meet the expectations. He's developed a facial tic, which suggests that anxiety may be affecting him on a physical level. Do you want Adam to have a contented life—or do you merely want him to have a superficial appearance of being successful, but wind up a self-critical, angry person with emotional problems?*

Tough questions like these usually help parents realize that they need to make major changes in their attitudes and expectations. Adam's parents, unfortunately, were not able to do this. After two sessions with me, they decided to seek advice elsewhere, still hoping to keep Adam in the same school.

Pushing a child to achieve beyond his capacity is a familiar example of unrealistic expectations. Here are some others:

- Asking a very shy child to be friendly
- Expecting a nine-year-old with no particular interest in music to sit through an adult concert
- Getting annoyed when a youngster says he's not tired and can't fall asleep at the hour the parent considers appropriate

I'm not suggesting that you go to the other extreme and expect too little of your child—that can turn into a self-fulfilling prophecy in which the youngster never attains her potential. But I don't believe in holding the carrot too far in front of the horse. Encourage a child to stretch, by all means, but don't burden her with unattainable goals.

How can you tell if you're expecting too much of your child? Here are possible signs:

- Your child often fails to live up to your expectations; you frequently are disappointed in her.
- The youngster signals that your expectations are unrealistic. He

might say things like, "I'm trying my best, but I just can't" or "I'm not doing it on purpose."

- Other people—such as your spouse, the child's teacher, or close friends—tell you that your standards are too high.

GIVE YOUR CHILD THE BENEFIT OF THE DOUBT

Part of the change to a more accepting attitude is making benign assumptions about your child's motives. I believe that virtually all children really want to please their parents. They don't feel victorious when they "win" battles with their mother and father; at best they are conflicted, and usually they're unhappy.

When parents don't understand the reason for a child's actions, they may assume that she's being annoying or difficult on purpose. If they recognize what's behind the behavior, they will find it easier to accept.

Sandra's mother and stepfather consulted me because of conflict between the girl, who was four, and her stepfather. He told me that Sandra had been spoiled by her mother and that the girl resented him. He described his stepdaughter as manipulative and said, "Whenever we go out together, she tries to humiliate me." As an example, he described a recent scene on the checkout line at a discount store. Sandra asked for candy; since they were on their way to lunch, he refused. She begged and whined; he told her angrily to stop. She began crying so loudly that other shoppers stared; some made critical comments. One of the onlookers, an elderly woman, gave Sandra a mint, and she stopped crying immediately.

An important part of my intervention was explaining that the girl's tantrums were not always manipulative.

ST: *You mentioned that you were on your way to lunch that day, so I assume Sandra was hungry.*

STEPFATHER: *Definitely. We were running late, and we'd had an early breakfast.*

ST: *And maybe she was tired from shopping.*

STEPFATHER: *We were both worn-out and hungry at that point.*

ST: *It's understandable that a four-year-old might behave badly simply because she's tired and hungry. Part of your distress at her behavior comes from a belief that it expresses hostility toward you, but that wasn't the case here.*

STEPFATHER: *Okay. Maybe that one time it wasn't really deliberate. But what about all the other times, when it's clear she's just being manipulative?*

ST: *You and your wife can tell her, in a planned discussion, that if she wants something and asks you politely she may get it; but if she's rude, she will* never *succeed. Then if she throws a tantrum, both of you must stand firm.*

STEPFATHER: *I can't always tell if she's carrying on because there's a real problem, or because she's trying to control me. What do I do about that?*

ST: *Believe me, I couldn't always tell the difference either. But when you're not sure, make the more charitable assumption. Don't worry about being manipulated—that's more your issue than hers.*

Acceptance does *not* mean tolerating rudeness and misbehavior or ignoring mistakes. As a parent, you must instruct your child. But it's possible to correct and direct in a neutral manner, without making the youngster feel bad.

Try to avoid criticizing your child when you are angry. Let me say at once: It's not always possible! If your child misbehaves, stop her and even punish her on the spot. But postpone any discussion until later, when emotions have cooled down. It's easy to be overcritical when you're angry. Even if you're in control, your child won't be receptive to constructive suggestions if she's upset. You'll be more effective as a teacher if you correct your child during a planned discussion, when you've had time to think about priorities and goals, and both of you are calm.

RESPECT YOUR CHILD'S PREFERENCES

Children's likes and dislikes should be honored if possible, even if they are unconventional. Families can get caught up in chronic conflicts when parents lose perspective and attempt to impose their own preferences in areas like clothing, food, friends, and activities. Often, when they back off and are more respectful of the child's wishes, she becomes much more flexible.

Particularly vulnerable to such struggles are children who are highly sensitive to tastes, smells, textures, and colors—especially if parents take issue with their choices. A finicky child, who insists on wearing the same few comfortable outfits all the time, might have recurring arguments with fashion-conscious parents who required her to dress "appropriately." But these conflicts wouldn't occur if the very same youngster had a mother and father to whom style wasn't important.

Nutrition-aware parents sometimes get into unproductive power struggles about eating. Jackson, age eight, upset his mother by refusing to eat breakfast. She had reason for concern: Jackson was small for his age, though his doctor had assured her that he was well within normal range. Also, the boy's teacher had told her that his behavior often deteriorated in the hour before lunch and that he complained of being hungry.

His mother described a typical morning: "I ask Jackson what he wants for breakfast, and he'll say something like 'Chocolate cake.' I tell him it has to be nutritious, and he says, 'A hot dog.' This goes on and on. Maybe eventually he agrees to have some cereal. So I get it ready, he takes one spoonful, and then he says he's full. So I try to get him to take some more, and pretty soon there's a big fight. Sometimes he goes off to school with no breakfast; sometimes I give up and let him eat whatever he wants, even if it's just a bag of potato chips."

Food was only one arena for struggles between Jackson and his mom, a single parent. She told me that he bullied her, that she didn't know how to stand up to him. Even though Jackson seemed to be "winning" most of the battles, he was an unhappy child who bit his fingernails, often until they bled.

His mother and I agreed that she should first tackle their problem concerning breakfast:

ST: *I suggest you have a planned discussion with Jackson and acknowledge that things haven't been going very well. Admit that you've been making matters worse by asking him to eat things he doesn't like. Explain that from now on you're going to respect his preferences about breakfast, and that the two of you will plan his morning menus together.*

MOTHER: *I don't think that will work. He'll just demand pizza or something else ridiculous.*

ST: *Well, pizza is nutritious. Why not let him have it?*

MOTHER: *But that would be giving in to him yet again!*

ST: *Not at all. You aren't giving in when you arrive at a decision during a planned discussion. It's not a situation in which you've been worn down by an argument just before school, and you say "yes" simply to get him off your back.*

Despite her misgivings, she followed my suggestion. As often happens, Jackson responded more reasonably than she had expected. When she asked him to propose a weekly breakfast menu, he took the assignment very seriously and came up with several ideas—including a "sundae" of granola and frozen yogurt—that were unconventional but nutritionally acceptable to his mother. There was an immediate improvement in their mornings, which gradually spread to other areas of their life. At a follow-up visit six months later, Jackson's mother told me that he was doing much better at school and at home.

RECRUIT YOUR CHILD'S STRENGTHS

When children are having problems, it's only natural for parents to focus on correcting their weak points. Often, however, it's much more productive to concentrate on building up strengths.

Martha was having a miserable time in fourth grade. She was a shy child and vulnerable to teasing; the class bully reduced her to tears almost every day. Her two best friends from the previous year had moved away. Martha hadn't made any new friends because her shyness and unhappiness made her unattractive to classmates. The teacher, though sympathetic, was going through a difficult pregnancy and was absent too often to provide consistent support.

Martha's parents tried to help her. They told her to ignore the bully and walk away; they encouraged her to act more friendly and to invite other girls to play. But nothing helped, and Martha became increasingly unhappy. Her parents consulted me when she became very reluctant to go to school.

I pointed out that although their advice was generally sensible, it really wasn't practical for Martha. "You're trying to get her to behave in a way that's not natural for her," I told them. "Instead, let's see what we might accomplish by focusing on her strengths."

When the parents turned their attention to their daughter's strong points, several promising ideas emerged. Martha was naturally graceful and had asked to take ballet lessons; her parents decided to enroll her in a neighborhood dance class. She was an avid and sensitive reader; this reminded them that the school librarian ran a "Junior Great Books" discussion group, and they arranged for her to join.

Participating in these activities was not the only intervention I suggested; Martha's parents also worked with her teacher and guidance counselor to improve the school environment. But focusing on strengths produced clear benefits. The positive comments of Martha's dance instructor helped boost her self-confidence. And she made several new friends in the book group, where she was seen in a more favorable light by other children.

SCHEDULE POSITIVE TIME TOGETHER

There's no clearer way to convey acceptance and respect than to spend predictable time with your child. I do not mean that you need to spend hours at a stretch or plan a series of "quality" cultural activities. What is essential is to let your child know that he can count on having your undivided attention regularly.

Predictability and fun are far more important than the specific activities and the amount of time spent. As with an exercise regimen, it's better to build a little into each day than to make up for chronic neglect with an occasional all-out effort. Even fifteen minutes—if it's a dependable fifteen minutes—can make a big difference.

Planning enjoyable activities to share is an important way for a parent and child to improve their relationship. This is rarely the only measure I suggest, but it's always helpful to have even brief periods in which things are good between you and the youngster.

Keith, age six, had lived with his mother while his parents went through a prolonged legal battle concerning their divorce. Eventually, custody was awarded to Keith's father and his new wife. By the time I saw them, not only the child but the adults, together and individually, needed considerable help.

One goal of treatment was to improve the relationship between Keith and his father. Keith was often hostile toward his father; at other times he was overly dependent. He frequently provoked his dad by attention-seeking behavior, such as whining or acting silly. Among other things, I suggested that the father establish a specific time each day when he and Keith did something pleasant together.

Some parents (Keith's were among them) initially resist the idea of planned rather than spontaneous interaction among family members; or they are concerned that too much time will be required and that the commitment will be inconvenient. I told Keith's dad: "Children thrive on predictability. The youngster who can rely on attention from a parent—perhaps over an unhurried early morning breakfast, or at bath- or bed-time—is less likely to cling and demand at inopportune moments."

Since Keith's father and stepmother were planning to buy him a dog, they decided that the father would keep Keith company when he took the dog on its evening walk. These excursions, which father and son both enjoyed, were a strong first step in a new direction. Within a few weeks, the father was accompanying Keith on morning dog walks as well. Though Keith's dad never used these pleasant times together for

planned discussions, he found that talking about sensitive issues afterward, when both of them were in a good mood, was very effective.

EXPECT APPROPRIATE INDEPENDENCE

Expecting too little of your child, just like expecting too much, is a kind
of nonacceptance. Low expectations can take the form of overprotect-
ing, babying, or not giving your child privileges, responsibilities, and
privacy appropriate to her age.

Sometimes parents overprotect out of anxiety: A nervous mother
might refuse to let her ten-year-old daughter ride a bicycle for fear of an
accident. Depending on the girl's nature, she might respond by fighting
her mother's restrictions; or she could become anxious herself. Over-
protected youngsters may have separation anxiety even to the point of
refusing to go to school.

While you do have to provide extra support for a youngster with
special needs, it's possible to go too far. Ira was born with missing fingers
on both hands. When he was seven, his parents still saw him as fragile
and incapable of caring for himself. His mother cut up his food and
bathed and dressed him; she remained in the room when other children
visited and overinstructed the other parents when he was a guest elsewhere. Ira was rude and tyrannical: He expected his family to respond
instantly to his demands.

When Ira's family attended a picnic sponsored by a support group
for parents of children with disabilities, they were astonished to see what
other youngsters in the group could accomplish. But when they tried to
persuade Ira to dress himself, he refused and accused them of not loving
him.

At my suggestion, the parents came up with a limited number of
new expectations and presented them to Ira in a planned discussion.
They told Ira that he was now old enough to dress himself and that he
could select his own outfits. He argued with them: "But you know I can't
do buttons! Will you make me go to school with my pants open?"

His parents reassured him. "We'll help with the buttons if you try and you really can't, but we think you're old enough and smart enough to do it yourself," his father said.

Ira was easily frustrated, and the first morning was a struggle. His mother was so upset to see her son fumbling unsuccessfully and in tears that her husband sympathetically suggested she leave the room and let him handle Ira's dressing. Within a few days, Ira had stopped complaining and was making a real effort to learn how to button his clothing. The situation improved considerably over the next few months. Ira and his parents took pride in his new accomplishments; as he became more independent, his demanding behavior decreased.

DON'T CARRY PRAISE TO EXCESS

Excessive criticism clearly represents a lack of acceptance. Less obvious is the nonacceptance conveyed by apparently doting parents who attempt to boost their child's self-esteem with what I call **self-image commercials:** They repeatedly say things like, "You're wonderful" or "You're a terrific kid." But exaggerated praise, like exaggerated criticism, can pressure a youngster and undermine her sense of who she really is.

Compliments that are out of line with a child's accomplishments or abilities ("You're a genius!") make her doubt her own perceptions. Far from making her confident, flattery tells her that her true self isn't enough. In extreme cases, she may become a perpetually dissatisfied perfectionist, who unsuccessfully struggles to live up to the idealized person her parents told her she was.

How can you tell you're going overboard with praise? Listen to yourself. And even more important, pay attention to your child's reactions:

- Does she seem pleased when you express pleasure and appreciation—or does she often look uncomfortable or even annoyed?

- Is she eager to hear what you have to say—or does she frequently cut you off with words like, "Stop making such a big deal."

■   ■   ■   ■

As acceptance increases, many beneficial changes result. Reasonable expectations interrupt the pattern of misbehavior and criticism. You begin to take pleasure in your child and feel better about yourself as a parent; the youngster's self-esteem improves. Parents are often surprised that a seemingly minor shift in attitude can make such a significant difference. They frequently tell me something like this: "It's not that I'm doing anything radically different; but I'm more relaxed and friendly, so my daughter is calmer, and there just aren't as many problems."

NINE

RETHINKING DISCIPLINE

It has never been easy to raise a child, and in some ways it's harder than ever. More parents are single; more mothers are employed outside the home. Often families are under multiple pressures and worn thin. Discipline advice from experts can be confusing: "Tough love" seems firm, but maybe too harsh; "active listening" is kinder, but does it really work?

For many parents, the very word "discipline" conjures up an image of sternness and punishment. But in fact, the term comes from the Latin word for learning. Indeed, I regard effective discipline as a very positive concept, in the same category as loving, respecting, and accepting a child.

Chronically ineffective discipline, on the other hand, can contribute to emotional problems. Persistent conflict erodes your child's relationship with you and gradually affects the way he feels about himself. Let me clarify that children aren't harmed by isolated instances of inadequate discipline or an occasional overindulgence or overreaction.

What's detrimental, as you'll see in the examples below, is a *persistent pattern* that becomes the family's usual way of operating.

Even if your child's emotional problems don't involve misbehavior, better discipline—like increased understanding and acceptance—is always helpful. This chapter helps you evaluate yourself as a disciplinarian and identify areas in need of change. That undoubtedly will generate many ideas and also will prepare you for Chapter 10, which offers new approaches to strengthening discipline.

HOW DOES YOUR CHILD KNOW YOU'RE SERIOUS?

Many conscientious parents find themselves unable to establish effective authority. Here are some of the explanations I hear:

> *"I'm afraid of hurting her feelings or damaging her self-esteem."*
> *"When I get home from work, I'm too exhausted to fight."*
> *"I know I indulge my child in some ways, but that's because I'm depriving him in others."*
> *"I see my kids only on weekends, and I want our limited time together to be as pleasant as possible."*
> *"The last thing I want to be is the kind of parent I had."*

How can you tell if you discipline effectively? It's simple: Ask yourself if your disciplinary methods generally produce lasting results in a manner you find acceptable. Whether your philosophy is democratic or autocratic, whatever techniques you use—reasoning, a "star" chart, time-outs, or spanking—**if it doesn't work, it's not effective**. This is true no matter how eminent the expert who recommended your approach, how reasonable it seems, or how successful it was with your other children or with you when you were a child.

One of the first questions I ask parents who consult me about behavior problems is: "How does your child know you're serious?" Usually they look at me as if I'm crazy and say things like this:

"I've told him a hundred times."

"She can see how angry I get."

"He's always being punished for that."

"I've explained it over and over again."

And then I tell them, "If you're responding this way so often, without having any effect, then something is wrong."

Marlene, age six, was stubborn, intense, and highly sensitive to sensory stimuli, especially touch. Her mother described her as "impossible." Most of their time together was spent arguing, and both were suffering as a result. Her mother described one area of conflict:

MOTHER: *She hates to take a bath. I've given up on the idea of a nightly bath, but I try to get her into the tub every few days. I've done all I can to make it pleasant: I read to her; she's got a dozen water toys—you name it. But the minute I announce that it's a bath night, there's a big battle.*

ST: *What happens when she refuses?*

MOTHER: *I usually get mad and scream at her. Sometimes she asks, "Why do I need a bath?" I explain, and we go round and round. Half the time she wears me out, and I just give up and send her to bed without the bath.*

ST: *This question may sound strange, but bear with me. How does Marlene know you're serious when you tell her she's supposed to take a bath?*

MOTHER: *You must be kidding! I just told you how I scream at her.*

ST: *Screaming doesn't indicate serious intent. Far more effective would be for you to decide ahead of time how often Marlene should bathe. Then talk to her when both of you are calm and give her a rule specifying when she takes a bath and what the consequences will be if she refuses. Adopt a much more matter-of-fact attitude.*

Like Marlene's mom, you may feel that you're constantly explaining, pleading, arguing, threatening, bribing, yelling, punishing, or losing your temper; and perhaps you also wind up backing down or feeling guilty. Parents sometimes say they're simply too tired to be good disciplinarians. But ineffective discipline also requires considerable effort, much of it quite unpleasant.

COMMON DISCIPLINE PROBLEMS

The questions below will help you take a detailed look at family discipline. As you will see, many discipline problems grow out of the best parental intentions. Simply identifying weak areas may suggest solutions.

ARE YOU TOO DEMOCRATIC?

Rachel is a bright and mature nine-year-old whose parents proudly explain that their daughter has been guided with reason, not simply commanded. She is consulted on all important family decisions. Recently, however, Rachel's mother has begun to wish she could have some time alone with her husband, instead of doing everything as a threesome. Both parents are distressed that Rachel has so few friends. Teachers have told them that other children find her too bossy.

Today, Rachel's parents are having a dinner party. As the adults gather at the table, Rachel pulls up a chair and sits down. Her father had explained earlier that this was an adults-only occasion. He tries to reason with her: "Rachel, dear, you've already had your supper. Now Mommy and I want to have dinner with our friends. When your friends visit you, you like to be alone with them, don't you? So please go to the den or to your room."

She says, "I want to be here. It's my house too, you know."

"This is no time for an argument," her mother tells her angrily.

Rachel remains in her chair, smiling sweetly. "I won't say a word," she promises. Her parents exchange irritated glances, then shrug their shoulders. Rachel helps herself to a roll.

In trying to be open and democratic with their children, some parents go too far. They give a child too much say in decisions that require adult judgment; they negotiate instead of taking a stand. This sends the message that there's no significant distinction between parent and child. Rachel's inappropriate role in her family makes her intrusive at home; it also may contribute to her bossiness at school.

Consider if democracy has gone too far in your family:

- Do you treat your child as an equal? Does she seem like an adult to you? If you have a bright, highly verbal youngster, it can be hard to remember that despite her sophisticated conversation, she's still a child.
- Do you expect respect and good manners?
- Do you insist on adult privacy? When your bedroom or bathroom door is closed, do your children enter without knocking?
- Do you hesitate to assert your authority? When your child disagrees with a decision of yours, do you feel obliged to explain your reasons to her satisfaction? Do you ask questions like, "What do you think your punishment should be?"

ARE ROUTINES AND EXPECTATIONS UNCLEAR?

Since her parents' divorce last year, seven-year-old Antonia has been whiny, clingy, and uncooperative. Her mother feels overwhelmed by her daughter's behavior, which comes on top of other unwelcome changes in her life. Mornings are especially difficult, because Antonia dawdles. When she misses the school bus—as happens at least twice a week—her mother must drive her, and then she's late for work. She has already received a warning from her boss.

Six-thirty one weekday morning, Antonia's mother wakes her up, puts a clean outfit on her chair, and tells her to get dressed. Fifteen minutes later, she returns to find Antonia playing with her Barbie doll, still wearing her pajamas. "Get dressed now," her mother says impatiently.

"In a minute," Antonia answers, not looking up.

"No—right now! I'm fed up with your dawdling!" shouts the mother. She snatches the Barbie from Antonia and points to the clothing on the chair.

Seven o'clock: Antonia is watching TV in the living room, wearing a stained T-shirt and jeans. "Take off that filthy shirt and put on the clothes I gave you!" her mother says angrily. She turns off the television and pushes Antonia toward the door.

Seven-twenty: Antonia is at the kitchen table, dressed but still barefoot. She refuses the bowl of cornflakes and milk her mother has prepared. The mother is furious. "Pick up that spoon this minute," she says. "The bus comes at seven-thirty, and I don't want you to be late again!"

Seven-twenty-five: Antonia reluctantly consumes a few spoonfuls of cereal while her mother hurriedly pulls on her socks and shoes. Before she can finish, the school bus passes.

The morning frustrations with Antonia are exacerbated by a lack of family structure. This harried mom faces each day as if it were a unique challenge. A routine would help her guide Antonia through the predictable steps of dressing and eating breakfast in time for the school bus. She also might remember that her daughter's irritating behavior is partly a reaction to the divorce and its consequences; therefore, her attitude could be more supportive.

Ask yourself if lack of structure might be a problem for your family:

- Are you always rushing? Do you often miss deadlines?
- Do you wait until the last minute to make decisions and tend to chores?
- Do you muddle through daily activities, rather than following routines? Do you often forget to do everyday tasks?
- Is your house generally disorganized and disorderly? Do you frequently lose things?

ARE YOU INCONSISTENT?

Brad is an eager-to-please twelve-year-old who is trying desperately to fit in at his new junior high. This stress, his father believes, explains why Brad has been uncharacteristically argumentative and fresh at home (especially with his mother), and has been neglecting his homework. Brad's mom thinks this is preteen rebelliousness that should be nipped in the bud. But his dad, who vividly remembers his own painful junior high school years, is very sympathetic. Brad's parents often argue about him; several weeks ago, they had a bitter quarrel after his mother grounded him for failing a social studies test.

Today, Brad and his father are shopping for jeans. "These are awesome!" says Brad, holding up a pair.

His father checks the price tag. "Sorry, Brad, but you know that Mom and I gave you a limit. This is way over. How about these?" He shows his son a similar pair that costs considerably less.

"I won't wear that dork brand," Brad responds scornfully. "This"—he points to the expensive jeans—"is the only pair I like."

His father reaches for his wallet. "I guess all rules have exceptions," he says. "We'll tell your mother there was a half-price sale." Father and son exchange conspiratorial smiles: This is not the first time they've put one over on Mom.

Brad's father is weakening parental authority by secretly undermining decisions made with his wife. Superficially, Brad seems pleased; but at a deeper level, his parents' quarrels about him are a source of guilt and anxiety.

Parents don't have to be completely consistent. Disagreements are part of normal family life: Adults have different personalities and backgrounds, so they're bound to have different views occasionally. It's not necessarily a bad thing for one parent to have a reputation for being "the softie." Even if parents are divorced, and there are different family rules at Mom's house and Dad's place, most youngsters can accommodate—so long as the divorced parents aren't undermining each other.

Inconsistency *is* a problem if parents view the child very differently, or if their expectations constantly shift. A youngster can become confused and insecure if he doesn't know what's expected of him. Also potentially harmful are discrepancies that reflect ongoing parental conflict.

Minor inconsistencies, which wouldn't trouble most youngsters, can be disruptive for a temperamentally difficult child. He will do best if the significant adults in his life coordinate their efforts and try to treat him the same way. If such a child must divide his time between two households, the rules and routines should be kept as similar as possible.

Some questions to ask yourself to determine if inconsistency is a problem:

- Do you and your spouse argue a lot about discipline?
- Does your child frequently play the two of you against each other? Have you become entrenched in good cop–bad cop roles? Do you say things like, "Don't tell your father about this; he'd have a fit."
- Are you inconsistent yourself? Do you change your mind about rules and the consequences for breaking them? Do you often make exceptions to your own rules?
- Do you get so angry that you feel guilty—and then you're too lenient the next time your child misbehaves?

ARE YOU BEWILDERED BY YOUR CHILD?

John's mother and father have a library of parenting books and devote nearly all their spare time to their son, who is four. He doesn't match the descriptions in their books; his behavior is confusing and unpredictable. One day he's ravenous; the next day he refuses to eat. Sometimes he won't go to bed and stays awake past midnight; other times he's exhausted by six. He gets upset easily, often for no apparent reason, and has long temper tantrums. His parents feel baffled and inadequate.

The father has taken John to the playground, which he usually enjoys. John wants to ride on a swing, but all the seats are taken. His father suggests the slide instead, and John reluctantly agrees. But that too is occupied. John becomes angry. His father tries to soothe him. John begins to cry.

The father sits down on the sidewalk, gathers John into his arms, and attempts to console him. By now John is sobbing loudly. A crowd gathers and the comments begin: "What did you do to him?" "Is he hurt?" "A child doesn't cry like that for no reason." "Why don't you help him?" John's father closes his eyes and rocks his son.

Discipline problems don't necessarily originate with parents. Not all youngsters are equally easy to deal with: A flexible child is easier than a stubborn one; a boy with regular eating and sleeping habits readily adjusts to family routines, while his younger sister battles her parents' efforts to impose consistent meal- and bed-times. The more temperamentally difficult the child, the more unpredictable his behavior is likely to be.

If a child's behavior is erratic, it's all too easy for his parents to become inconsistent as well. But parents of such a youngster—even more than other mothers and fathers—need to stand back and evaluate his behavior. Once they understand the role of temperament, they become more sympathetic and less worried. Often they can find ways to avoid—or at least minimize—the problems.

Here are some questions to help you see if your child might be harder-than-average to discipline:

- Does your child have many of the difficult temperamental traits described in Chapter 6?
- Is your child unpredictable?
- Do you feel confused by his or her behavior?
- Do disciplinary techniques work one day and become useless the next?

If you have an innately hard-to-raise youngster, you will find many specific suggestions in my first book, *The Difficult Child*.

Do You Spoil Your Child?

The unspoken rule at Wendy's house is: "She gets whatever she wants." That includes unlimited attention and tolerance, as well as expensive toys. But even Wendy's parents, much as they love their pampered five-year-old daughter, are worn-out by her incessant demands. Moreover, they're concerned by complaints from her teacher that she is fresh and disobedient.

The family is playing a game of Chutes and Ladders. If Wendy draws a card that would send her down a chute, she demands to put it back and take another. Her parents permit this, rather than upset her. But now her father gets a good ladder and unexpectedly wins. "That's not fair!" she howls. She bursts into tears and knocks the pieces on the floor. The mother throws her arms around Wendy to comfort her, while her father scrambles to pick up the game.

An overindulged child is vulnerable to emotional problems. When a youngster is demanding, parents often get angry and overreact. Such overreaction (or other parental mistakes) makes them feel guilty, which in turn leads to further overindulgence. Other forms of guilt also lead to spoiling: A working mom may feel guilty about the time and attention she gives to her job; a depressed dad may berate himself for upsetting his child.

Parents may be reluctant to impose limits on children who get upset easily. It's fine to be somewhat indulgent when a child is acutely distressed, but nearly all youngsters are able to comply with normal family rules most of the time. I sometimes have to remind excessively concerned parents that their "poor little girl" seems to be perfectly capable of controlling her behavior in school and at Grandma's house. Therefore, they could expect a little more from her.

Youngsters who aren't taught to accept limits at home may be unable to accept them anywhere else. Spoiled children can become self-centered, excessively bossy with their peers and, like Wendy, disrespectful of teachers.

As you probably have observed in other families, parents are often the last to know that their child is spoiled! Look for patterns, not isolated incidents, as you ask yourself these questions:

- Is your child bossy? Does she tell you what to do?
- If she wants something badly, does she usually get it? When you try to set limits, can she wear you down by whining or wheedling?
- Is your child frequently rude or demanding? Does she usually omit "please" and "thank you"? Does she feel free to interrupt

you when you're on the telephone, working, or talking with another adult?

- Are you overindulging your child materially? Do you deprive yourself of necessities to give her luxuries?
- Do other people tell you she's spoiled?

ARE YOU TOO STRICT?

The downstairs neighbors occasionally complain that Scott, age eight, makes too much noise. His father posts notes all around the apartment reminding Scott about the rules for being quiet: "Take off your shoes when you come in." "Keep the TV volume low enough so it can't be heard in the next room." "Don't run in the house." When Scott forgets a rule, which happens at least once a day, his father gets angry and takes twenty-five cents off his allowance. Some weeks he gets no allowance at all.

Scott looks around nervously as he enters his house; he blinks rapidly. His school bag slides off his shoulder, and he cringes at the sound it makes when it hits the floor. His mother comes running. "Scott! Try to be more careful!" she says, sounding annoyed.

"I didn't do it on purpose," he tells her sadly. "I really want to be quiet."

A child may be subject to rules he can't follow and punished for behavior he can't help. That could happen because his parents believe they themselves ultimately benefited from the strict discipline imposed on them as kids. They say things like, "I had the devil knocked out of me, and I'm glad" or "I really learned my lesson."

Nearly every parent is overly strict on occasion, so when you answer the questions below, look for persistent patterns:

- Does your family have too many rules? Do you frequently announce new regulations? Does your child seem genuinely confused about what he's supposed to do?
- Are your rules too restrictive? Does your child complain about them a lot? Do you sometimes feel trapped by your own rules?

- Can your child really obey your rules? Is he old enough? Does he have enough self-control?
- Do your attitudes about child-rearing lead you to be overly demanding? These are statements I often hear from parents who over-discipline:

"I believe in striving for perfection—why settle for anything less than the best?"
"Too much praise can go to a child's head."
"If I make a rule, I don't make exceptions."
"Spare the rod, spoil the child."

- Your child is chronically anxious, angry, or sad, and makes comments that point to excessive strictness. Here's what overdisciplined kids commonly say to me: "I never get anything right." "My dad is always mad at me."
- Do other people warn you that you're too harsh, or that your standards are too high?

WHY PARENTS MUST CHANGE FIRST

When parents consult me about a child's behavior problems, they usually assume that improvements must begin with the child. They see themselves as merely reacting to misbehavior. My job is to help them realize that their own responses are actually contributing to the problem behavior.

The specifics vary, of course, but when I ask parents to describe a typical incident, it usually sounds something like the account below from the mother of a ten-year-old girl:

ST: *You've told me that Jessica is stubborn and argumentative. Can you give me an example?*

MOTHER: *Okay. Last night was typical. I told Jessica to do her math homework, and she said, "I'll do it later." That means*

*"never"—she's a procrastinator. So I told her, "No. Do it now."
She started complaining that it's boring. I said, "Homework
doesn't have to be exciting."*

*Then she asked, "Why does anyone need to know arithmetic
when you can use a calculator?" I've heard that line dozens of
times, so I got angry and said, "Don't ask 'Why?'—just do it!"*

She said, "I will not!"

*We went back and forth some more. Finally I got fed up. I
told her she can flunk math for all I care. Then I went to my
room, slammed the door, and tried to read.*

When parents and children go through the very same steps over and
over again, each move in their troubled tango leads to the next: The
child's act triggers an admonition or punishment from the parent; this
negative response prompts the youngster to move to the next stage of
misbehavior.

As I've already emphasized: **The adults must change first.** My
advice is to tear up the familiar script, which sabotages the child by
perpetuating conflict and failure.

Jessica's mother already knew that she and her daughter were stuck.
By the time she had finished her recital of the previous evening's events,
we both were laughing.

> ST: *Perhaps next time you should skip the pointless discussion.
> Go to your room and slam the door right away.*
>
> MOTHER: *I know you're kidding, but I'm ready to try any-
> thing!*
>
> ST: *Let's be serious now: This pattern of daily arguments should
> be completely eliminated. I suggest you seek Jessica's input in a
> planned discussion, then establish rules for homework, with
> clear penalties if she doesn't cooperate.*
>
> MOTHER: *Let's say we have a planned discussion and agree
> that eight o'clock is homework time. What do I do when it's
> eight o'clock and she gives me the same old arguments?*
>
> ST: *I often tell parents, "When your child asks you to dance,
> you don't have to accept." If she tries to pick a fight, don't*

answer in your usual way. Simply say, "You know the rule, Jessica. Eight o'clock is homework time." And if necessary, impose the penalty.

■   ■   ■   ■

Embattled parents come to view their child as someone who is trying to thwart them. They don't expect cooperation, so they look for ways to manipulate or hoodwink him. Fundamental to improving discipline is a major attitudinal shift: **Instead of viewing the youngster as an adversary, the parents become his allies.** This means seeing your child as a fundamentally decent little person whom you are trying to guide and help.

The next chapter offers my approach to improved family discipline, which rests on adult leadership and strategic planning. Rather than confronting each failure with more disapproval and punishment, the focus will be on improving the youngster's chances for success. Parents usually are greatly encouraged to learn that their own actions, which they can control, will make a significant difference.

TEN

DISCIPLINE THAT PROMOTES SUCCESS

This chapter will show you how to improve discipline and use it to solve problems. Effective discipline is founded upon three elements:

- Parental authority
- Structure
- Strategic reactions

Perhaps these sound stern and rigid, but they really aren't. As I emphasized in Chapter 8, children's ideas and personal characteristics should be taken into account. Good discipline is always a blend: kindness with firmness; parental leadership with the child's participation; structure with flexibility. The aim is not to fence a youngster behind dictatorial rules, but to create a system that will foster his or her success.

When parents consult me about a discipline problem, they usually are caught in on-the-spot responses to unacceptable behavior. They wait tensely for the child to misstep; sooner or later she does, and they react. In effect, the youngster controls the interaction. This makes parents feel ineffective and victimized, and erodes their sense of competence.

Effective discipline requires adult leadership and planning. Instead of relying on criticism and punishment to correct misbehavior after the fact, the parents' primary focus is on guiding the youngster and preventing difficulties. **One planned course of action is far more effective than endlessly repeated spontaneous reactions**.

In this chapter, you will see how planning is used to resolve emotional and behavioral problems. An underlying assumption is that success builds upon itself. Goals should be easily attainable. Even a reduced incidence of failure should be considered a form of success.

RECLAIM ADULT AUTHORITY

Families are not democracies. It should be clear to all members that the grown-ups are in charge. Most children—even adolescents—feel more secure when authority rests with the adults.

As we saw in Chapter 9, some parents undercut their own authority in an effort to be egalitarian. While children should have a say in matters that concern them, discipline is weakened when all family members are treated as equals.

ADULT-CHILD BOUNDARIES

Adult authority requires a boundary between the domains of adults and children in the family. This can be difficult for single parents or for a married parent whose spouse doesn't provide support and companionship. A single father of three may find it hard to resist pressing his mature nine-year-old daughter into service as a junior mother substitute for his five-year-old twins. The woman who is reeling from the discovery of her husband's infidelity may yearn to talk about her unhappiness with her sympathetic eleven-year-old son. But it's not good for a child to become an assistant parent or confidant. Children who are involved in adult concerns from an early age grow up too quickly and miss out on the joys of childhood.

Maintaining distinctions that suit your values as well as the needs of your child is a matter of balance. While I don't want to tell you how to lead your life, I can offer these general suggestions:

- *Children should not be privy to adult issues.* It's unfair to burden children with adult problems, such as marital difficulties or career setbacks. This is not to say that significant family matters must be kept secret; however, children should be given information appropriate to their age.

Suppose, for example, a mother has lost her job. She might explain to her five- and seven-year-old girls that the family will need to cut back on expensive clothing and activities, or ask them to cooperate with efforts to save money. But she shouldn't upset her daughters by sharing her fears about unemployment—that's an adult concern.

A clear sign that children are too involved in adult issues are comments indicating precocious awareness. For example, a six-year-old boy worries aloud if his parents can really afford the computer they bought for his birthday. Or a seven-year-old girl remarks to her mother, "It's nice that you and Daddy are getting along better now."

- *Adults should have time alone.* Today's busy parents—many of whom feel chronically guilty about how little time they spend with their children—often are reluctant to exclude them from their conversations and social activities. While all-family get-togethers and activities can be fun for everyone, parents are entitled to adults-only time as well. I'm always concerned when a mother and father tell me they just about never spend time alone together or go out as a couple. The consequences go beyond authority and discipline: Lack of adult privacy has obvious adverse effects on parents and their relationship.

- *Children also should have lives of their own.* Boundaries work both ways. Unless there is a specific reason for parents to be involved, they don't need to know every detail of a youngster's life—for instance, how a twelve-year-old boy spent his allowance, or the conversation topic that made two nine-year-old girls giggle. Respecting your child's boundaries is a way of expressing confidence in his ability to function independently.

■ *Family members are entitled to privacy.* In some homes, children have almost unlimited access to their parents. They are permitted to overhear and interrupt adult conversations; the door to the parents' bedroom or even bathroom is never closed.

I consider some degree of physical modesty desirable within the home, the specifics depending upon the culture and personal preferences of family members. I also believe that parents and children should have their own rooms, if possible, and that family rules should prohibit anyone from opening a closed door without knocking.

An absence of privacy often is at the heart of quarrels between siblings. Enforcing an older child's right to bar a younger one from her personal space and activities can do wonders for their relationship.

THE CHILD AS JUNIOR COLLABORATOR

The older the child, the more important is his input and cooperation with solutions. As you move away from an adversarial posture and create an alliance with your child, you want him to feel a sense of participation. At the same time, a youngster shouldn't be burdened by decisions that properly belong to adults, such as whether he should go to school—that's the difference between a junior collaborator and an equal partner.

Ultimately, your goal is to provide your child with the skills and confidence he needs to be an independent person, capable of overcoming his own problems. Some suggestions:

■ *Consult the child whenever possible.* A younger child can be given some say about the order of events in a bedtime routine; an older child can be involved in choosing after-school activities.

■ *Teach your own coping techniques to your child.* In modified form, they may be helpful to her as well. For example, I've found that parents who practice meditation can teach their children how to do it, with excellent results. Similarly, the relaxation techniques developed for adults by behavioral psychologists—including deep breathing, visualization, and progressive muscular relaxation—can be helpful for children who are anxious or fearful or who have poor impulse control.

USING PLANNED DISCUSSIONS

Chapter 4 described the planned discussion technique in detail and showed you how it can help parents talk about family issues and solicit a youngster's input. In this chapter, you will see how the same technique also is effective for introducing new routines, setting forth rules and consequences, and exploring methods for preventing misbehavior.

Here are some points to remember:

- *Adults should meet privately ahead of time to prepare for a planned discussion.* Try not to get distracted by mutual complaints. The point is to arrive at a joint plan not only for solving the problem, but also for conducting the planned discussion with the child. You can even decide who will talk and what words will be used. Though this kind of detailed planning may sound artificial, an unprepared presentation could be too general or rambling, and the child might misunderstand or stop paying attention.
- *Arrange for uninterrupted time.* During a planned discussion, you should not be doing anything else, such as watching TV or answering the telephone.
- *Create a formal atmosphere.* Call the child into the room and ask everyone to sit down.
- *Be brief, so the youngster's attention doesn't wander.*
- *Establish the right mood: not angry, but serious and firm.* The child has to sense that you mean what you say. I sometimes suggest that parents practice their demeanor in front of a mirror.
- *Seek the child's input.* However, everyone must understand that the adults have the final word.
- *Check that the child understands what's expected of her.* Ask her to repeat the instructions in her own words.

- *End the discussion by expressing your confidence in the youngster and asking her to do her best.* This is a powerful inducement, even with a seemingly rebellious youngster. Most children really do want to please their parents.

ESTABLISH A CLEAR FAMILY STRUCTURE

When I refer to family structure, I'm talking about order, predictability, consistency, routines, and clear rules and expectations. In general, the specific practices a family adopts are not as important as the fact that *some* structure is in place; youngsters can thrive under many diverse arrangements.

Structure isn't the same as rigidity. For example, if you have an established bedtime for your children, it doesn't have to remain the same on weekends or during vacations. You don't need to organize all parts of your life; nor does every child need a great deal of structure. Nevertheless, most people—adults as well as children—find reassurance and comfort in knowing that at least some of the events in their lives happen in predictable, consistent ways.

Order and predictability become especially important when a youngster has difficulties. Introduced strategically, structure can help solve specific problems. Here are some suggestions concerning structure that I made to a mother and father who were having nightly struggles with their twelve-year-old son, Bennett, over homework:

ST: *What kind of structure do you have for homework?*

MOTHER: *I'm not sure what you mean. He gets assignments every day in school, and he knows he's supposed to do them. We're constantly reminding him to do his homework, and we've told him to come to us if he has any problems. Isn't that enough?*

ST: *All that certainly would be enough for some children, but apparently it's not sufficient for Bennett. Do you have a specific time when he's supposed to work on assignments?*

FATHER: *Ideally, he should get a head start before dinner, then finish up afterwards. But that rarely happens.*

ST: *Perhaps you should make a rule specifying times for doing homework. Is there a particular place where Bennett is supposed to work on assignments?*

MOTHER: *We don't let him do homework in front of the TV, but otherwise it's up to him. The best place would be at the desk in his room, because he wouldn't be interrupted. Mostly he does it in the kitchen, though.*

ST: *Well, you might specify that he work at his desk, or you could plan that he work in the kitchen and arrange to minimize interruptions. You mentioned telling him that he can come to you with questions. Does he do that?*

FATHER: *Sometimes. What usually happens is that he puts it off. Then at the last minute, when he really should be getting ready for bed, he's frantic because he doesn't understand a math problem.*

ST: *That should happen less often when he's on a schedule. Part of the plan could be that you're available to help him at an agreed-upon time.*

FATHER: *I see what you mean by structure.*

PROCEDURES AND ROUTINES

One way to enhance structure is to establish procedures—standard ways of doing things within the family. These are useful for solving recurring conflicts and problems. Families benefit whenever a stressful, disorganized situation can be replaced by order. Predetermined behavior patterns cut down on friction, since they reduce the number of discussion and decision points. Once established, they become habits and are carried out automatically. Your family probably has some procedures in place already.

While you don't want to choreograph your child's every move, consider creating procedures when the benefits of order and predictability seem to outweigh the advantages of spontaneity. Obvious candidates for this kind of structure include: getting ready in the morning, preparing meals, doing chores and homework, arranging for a child to have daily private time with a parent, and winding down at the end of the day.

One kind of procedure is a **routine**—a predictable sequence of prescribed events. Perhaps the most common example is the bedtime routine. For a young child this might consist of taking a bath, changing into pajamas, watching TV, then getting into bed, listening to a story, and finally receiving a good-night kiss from each parent. There could be some variation in the time allotted to TV if there is a special show, or in the length of the story, but if it's a routine, these events would always occur in the same order.

A routine was helpful with Angela, a five-year-old girl whose parents consulted me because of problems at bedtime. Her mother was spending more than an hour each night putting Angela to bed: She read her stories, fetched drinks, and finally lay down next to her until she fell asleep. If the mother tried to leave earlier, Angela burst into tears and screamed that she was scared. Though her nominal bedtime was seven-thirty, her mom usually remained in the room until after nine.

I suggested that Angela's parents devise a new evening routine that would give their daughter plenty of loving attention, but place limits on what she could demand. Together they came up with a system, which they presented to her during a planned discussion.

Angela's parents described the new arrangement in positive terms. Her father said, "Since you are a big girl, from now on your bedtime will be eight o'clock, instead of seven-thirty." He explained the routine, which began with a bath at six-forty-five and ended after stories with her mother. At eight each night, her mom would turn on the night light and leave the room.

The routine worked well for several nights, but only until the mother's departure. Angela would burst into tears when her mother tried to leave. "I'm scared!" she cried. "Don't go away!"

Clearly, an additional strategy was needed, but the parents disagreed about what to do. We discussed the situation:

FATHER: *My wife spoils Angela. That's the problem right there. I tell her, "Just let her cry. In a couple of days, she'll see you mean business, and she'll go to bed without a peep."*

MOTHER: *Part of me agrees with him. I know she's probably just being manipulative. But at the same time, I'm really worried. She clings to me; her whole body trembles. It would be heartless to leave her alone if she's really terrified.*

ST: *There's no question: You should be there for your child. Don't worry about being manipulated; assume she's being genuine with you when she says she's afraid. It's always appropriate to adopt an emotionally generous posture toward a child. But you can give her support and at the same time limit your involvement at bedtime.*

MOTHER: *I don't see how I can do both—if I stay, I'm involved; if I leave, I'm not supportive.*

ST: *Remain in the room, by all means, to help Angela cope with her fears. But this is not a time for socializing: Don't talk to her, and don't let her talk to you. Just sit in a chair in another part of the room. You can bring a lamp and read.*

MOTHER: *I know she'll talk to me. What am I supposed to do then, ignore her?*

ST: *Tell her in another planned discussion that you want to help, but that she has only two choices: If she's quiet, you'll stay in the room. But if she talks to you, she'll have to be alone with the door closed. And you must be prepared to follow through. If Angela attempts to engage you in conversation, take a deep breath, walk out, close the door, and hold it closed.*

MOTHER: *That's what my husband says—let her scream.*

ST: *For how long do you think I'm suggesting that you keep the door closed?*

MOTHER: *I don't know.*

ST: *Keep the door closed for twenty seconds. The idea is not to frighten Angela into submission, but to make it clear that you're serious. After twenty seconds, open the door, take her into the living room, and help her calm down. Then say, "You see, I meant what I said. Let's go back to the room and try again." Your attitude should be kind but not overly sympathetic.*

Clarifying the distinction between overindulging her daughter and being available to meet a true emotional need helped Angela's mother remain firm. The bedtime routine became established and, as often happens, the situation improved rapidly. Within a few weeks, the fears dissipated, and the mother was able to leave Angela after saying good night.

EXPECTATIONS AND RULES

As you know by now, I don't believe in telling parents just what they should require from their children: Specific expectations depend upon the family's own culture and style. But whatever you want from your child, make your expectations clear. Children become anxious when they don't really know what's expected of them. Unclear expectations also lead to parental inconsistency.

Children learn most social and family expectations without explicit lessons. They observe others; they're taught and corrected as they go about their lives. But sometimes this casual process must be supplemented by more formal instruction.

If a child's behavior is not satisfactory, the first step is to articulate your expectations clearly, even if you think they're obvious. Children don't necessarily know what you mean when you say "Be good" or "Act nice." Often, a more precise expression of your wishes is sufficient. If not, the next step is to turn the expectation into a family rule. Rules may be backed up with consequences, positive or negative, for compliance or noncompliance. Whenever possible, a child should not be punished unless the expectation, rule, and consequence are clearly articulated ahead of time.

Parents can't regulate every aspect of a child's life. If you constantly declare new rules, that's a sign of trouble. It's better to announce one rule, and have the child obey it, than to have six rules that are enforced inconsistently. Persistent disobedience also signals that something isn't working.

If that happens, start over: Present explicit rules in a planned discussion, even if you have repeatedly chastised the child for the misbehavior. The same statement carries far more weight if you and the youngster are calm, and the discussion takes place away from any incident. Here's an example:

Julian, age four, was ruining dinner with demanding, disgusting behavior. If food failed to please him, he would spit it out and whine until his parents prepared something else. They had lectured him about table manners, and punished him by sending him out of the room and taking away television privileges, but their responses were not consistent.

When I suggested a planned discussion to explain to Julian that he was not allowed to spit out food, his mother was puzzled. She said, "What's the point? He already knows that: Every time he does it, we tell him how revolting it is." Obvious as a no-spitting-at-the-table rule might seem to an adult, a child's perceptions could be different. Despite their expressions of disapproval, Julian's parents had never presented him with a *rule* that carried specific consequences for disobedience. And it didn't help that they had unwittingly rewarded the behavior by preparing a new dish when he did it.

During the planned discussion, Julian's mother said, "From now on there's a new rule in this house: Nobody can spit out food during dinner. Daddy and I want to eat with you, but if you spit, you will have to leave the table and eat by yourself in the kitchen, with no TV."

For the first week after the planned discussion, Julian's parents reminded him about the rule just once before they sat down for dinner. (I had warned them that over-reminding could be counterproductive.) On the second night, Julian protested that he didn't like the applesauce because it was "too lumpy," but he didn't spit it out. For Julian, this kind of complaint represented real progress. But a few evenings later, he spit out a chunk of stew, saying it was "too spicy." His parents, calmly and without expressions of disgust, sent him away from the table. This minor setback was followed by substantial improvement.

PLAN YOUR REACTIONS
TO MISBEHAVIOR

Improved family structure will greatly cut down the frequency of confrontations with your child. Nevertheless, part of planning is deciding
ahead of time how to deal with the inevitable incidents of misbehavior.
Planning and practice will allow you to react more quickly and effectively, and with less anger and distress. Many kinds of reactions can be
planned.

EARLY INTERVENTION

Problem behavior often is preceded by warning signs. If you can learn to
recognize them, you may be able to prevent recurrent difficulties. Use a
planned discussion with the child to explain preventive interventions.
This prepares him for your actions, and also teaches him how to control
his own behavior.

Kevin, age eight, frequently lost control while playing and pushed or
hit other children. His parents asked me, "What can we do when he's
mean?" I encouraged them to think about the situation differently. This
was an easily excited child who was impulsive rather than mean. His
parents hovered over him, but they didn't act until he actually struck
out. Then they responded with a lecture or punishment.

When I prodded their memories, they realized that Kevin displayed
several warning signs before he became overstimulated: He generally
began to talk louder, he moved more quickly, and he giggled in a
distinctive way. I suggested that they use this information to step in
earlier.

The specific intervention I recommended was the **nonpunitive
time-out:** moving an excited youngster to more quiet surroundings.
Unlike an ordinary time-out, used as an after-the-fact punishment, this
helps a child calm down. The adult is sympathetic; the child does not
have to be isolated or deprived of privileges—he can read, watch TV, or
socialize quietly.

I suggested that Kevin's parents have a planned discussion with him to explain what they would be doing. It's important to let him know that the time-out is not a punishment, but a way of helping him. Part of a collaborative approach is teaching Kevin about himself and pointing out signs of overexcitement that he can watch for. Ideally, Kevin will learn to give himself a time-out when he senses that his control is slipping.

DELIBERATE NONREACTION

Sometimes, the most effective parental reaction is no reaction. You may be able to do nothing; you may be able to wait. There are good reasons to hold back:

- *A parental response, even if negative, carries the "reward" of attention.* Thus you may unintentionally reinforce the very behavior you're trying to stop. Nonreaction is a useful technique for dealing with irritating behavior, such as whining or pestering, which so often is fueled by the parent's negative response. Matter-of-factly going about your business is often more effective than getting drawn into a protracted no-win situation. If this doesn't work, you can adopt a different strategy later on.

Sometimes the parent of an argumentative child tells me, "I can't ignore him, because he keeps talking." I suggest saying something brief like, "Nothing more remains to be said." If the father has been dealing with the child, he could ask his wife to take over; he could leave the room; or he could simply pick up a magazine and turn his attention to that.

When I advise a parent to ignore behavior, I don't mean they should pretend it isn't happening. Obviously, if the child is hurting someone or destroying things, that must be stopped. But after a simple action or statement, the parent should withdraw emotionally, and perhaps physically, from the situation.

- *Overly rapid adult intervention can prevent the child from developing his own ways of coping.* The first time I saw Bernard, age seven, he was slightly nervous. When I asked him to come into my office, he hesitated briefly. Instead of waiting to see if he'd step forward on his own, his mom launched a barrage of reassurances: "This is the nice doctor I told you about, the one who's going to help you. Now you don't have to worry, Bernard, because he isn't going to hurt you." As she went on and on, Bernard became visibly anxious.

Many caring parents don't realize that their premature involvement in fact increases the problem. If you tend to hover over your child, try to ask yourself before intervening: Could I do nothing? Am I really needed? What could I lose by waiting a few moments? Such a pause by Bernard's mother would have allowed him to overcome his slight nervousness on his own.

- *Not reacting can improve the emotional climate of the family.* Occasionally during my first meeting with a family there isn't time for me to make all the specific suggestions they need. But if it's clear that power struggles are taking place, with parents and child stuck in a negative cycle of anger, disobedience, and overreactions, I simply tell them: "Between now and our next appointment, cut down by half the number of situations you respond to, and try to say 'Yes' more often than 'No.'" No matter what further measures are needed, this is bound to help.

RESPONDING QUICKLY AND CLEARLY

Once you've decided to respond to your child, it's best to do so quickly. A rapid "yes" is a decision; if delayed too long, and said after the child has begun to whine, it's giving in. Taking an early stand is especially important if a youngster is persistent and stubborn. Here's what happened when Avi—an accomplished negotiator at age six—spotted the pretzel jar in my office:

AVI: *Can I have a pretzel?*
ST: *You'll have to ask your mother.*
AVI: *Mom?*
MOTHER: *Sorry, Avi.*
AVI: *Why not?*

> MOTHER: *It's too close to dinnertime. I don't want you to lose your appetite.*
>
> AVI: *But when we were shopping yesterday, you let me have candy.*
>
> MOTHER: *That was an exception.*
>
> AVI: *Why can't today be an exception?*

The exchange went on and on, and finally she gave in. Later I explained to the mother—who, by the way, was an attorney!—that once she announces her decision, she should not reason interminably with Avi. Going on and on merely gets a stubborn child even more stuck. Instead, the discussion should be brought to an end as quickly and as firmly as possible.

I suggested that she have a planned discussion with Avi in which she said something like this: "From now on, I am not going to argue with you. I'll try to say 'yes' more often, but when I say 'no,' I mean it."

STOPPING THE BEHAVIOR

Sometimes a child's behavior must be interrupted. In that case, do so as quickly and calmly as you can. Try not to wait until you've lost your temper!

Parents sometimes tell me things like, "My child comes into my room when I'm busy, and I can't get him out" or "My child hits me, and I can't make him stop." The children in question are not burly teenagers, but boys and girls as young as three or four. I have to remind these parents that they are bigger, stronger, and smarter than their children, and that of course they can limit their behavior. A youngster who has invaded a parent's room can be physically removed; a child who is hitting can be restrained. I'm not suggesting that parents descend to the child's level and get into a fight; rather, they should simply limit the child physically. This is not punishment, and should be done as neutrally as possible.

REWARDS

Rewards can be helpful when you're trying to enhance family structure and encourage new behavior. But if they aren't used carefully, they can backfire. Parents who resort to rewards too frequently often are dismayed to discover that their children respond to every parental request with "What will you give me?"

The best rewards are the ones that follow naturally from good behavior. For example, a consequence of keeping toys orderly is that they're easier to find and less likely to get broken. Parents can build automatic rewards into a child's life. I always advise that bedtime or other routines be planned so that the most enjoyable parts are at the end. For instance, if TV is part of a child's weekday morning routine, it should come after the youngster gets dressed and eats breakfast, not before.

Planned rewards, whether natural or arranged, are useful for establishing new routines without unpleasantness. Introducing rewards also helps when you're in an entrenched situation with a child and are trying to move in a positive direction.

Glen, age nine, was an anxious child with a loving but demanding father. High on the father's list of irritants was Glen's nervous habit of biting his nails. One of my goals was to soften the father's attitude and make his relationship with Glen less adversarial. Accordingly, I suggested that he offer a reward to help the boy stop biting his nails. He strongly objected:

> **FATHER:** *I don't believe in bribery! Some of Glen's friends get five dollars for every "A" on their report card, and he knows what I think of that. If I bribe him to stop biting his nails, that would be inconsistent.*
>
> **ST:** *I'm not suggesting anything more than a token reward, such as taking Glen to a movie.*
>
> **FATHER:** *My other two kids—who never bit their nails— would be on my back for being unfair.*
>
> **ST:** *You can explain to them that Glen has a problem they don't*

have, and that you're trying to help him solve it. It is not unfair to treat each child as an individual.

FATHER: *I've always prided myself on sticking with principles. Assuming I decide to do this—and I'm still not sure about it— how do I explain it to Glen after everything I've said on the subject of bribes?*

ST: *Your son's nail biting has been one of the thorns in your relationship. Offering an inducement instead of scolding him would signal that you've made a fresh start and that you're on his side now. You might say something like this: "I know that habits are hard to break, and I want to help you stop biting your nails. We've been angry with each other about this for a long time, and I want us both to make a new start. So I'm giving you a little extra incentive."*

My thinking about rewards has evolved considerably since I wrote *The Difficult Child*, and I now recommend them much less often than before. I've found that unless parents make fundamental changes in acceptance and discipline, any improvements created by rewards are not long-lasting. It is the experience of success—the feeling of accomplishment and the pleasure of receiving parental approval—that is the true reward.

PUNISHMENT

I have put punishment at the end of this chapter because I deemphasize it in my approach to discipline. When parents come to me looking for more potent punishments, as if they were an antibiotic against misbehavior, what's really needed is a more effective system of adult authority and greater attention to planning.

As I said earlier, the first step in dealing with misbehavior is to make sure that the child understands what is expected of him. It's not fair to punish unless you have presented clear-cut rules that let the youngster know which behavior is not allowed and what will happen if he disobeys—something that can be communicated during a planned discussion. But if an explicit rule is broken, punishment should follow as swiftly as possible. Once you demonstrate your willingness to follow through, a mere warning usually suffices.

The consequences of misbehavior—whether intrinsic to the situation or arranged by parents—sometimes are punishment enough. Parents should explain these ahead of time. For instance, children who are too demanding can be told that they will *never* get what they want if they ask rudely; if they make a polite request, at least they have a chance.

Parents often ask me what type of punishment is most effective. Sometimes they're worried about possible adverse consequences of using particular punishments, especially spanking. While you must decide which specific punishments are most suitable for your family, here are some guidelines:

- *Punishments don't have to be harsh.* Your attitude is far more significant than the nature or severity of the penalty. Even seemingly "light" punishments—such as sending the child to his or her room for a short time, or withdrawing a privilege such as watching TV—are highly effective when you calmly and seriously make it clear that you mean business. Parents who threaten a child with dire consequences often become inconsistent: Either they calm down and decide not to follow through on overly severe punishments, or they penalize the child too heavily, feel guilty, and then try to compensate by overindulgence.

- *If you punish severely or frequently, that's a clear sign that a completely different approach is needed.* Punishment should be a seldom-used last resort, not the first technique you try in response to misbehavior.

What about spanking? While I don't advocate spanking, and never recommend it, I think it's ridiculous to speak about a swat on the rear as if it were child abuse.

- *To be effective, punishment should be prompt.* A single warning (but just one) can be helpful, especially to a child who is easily distracted and needs a reminder. Once you've established your authority, a stern "Cut that out right now!" often will suffice to get your child back in line. But don't erode your credibility by warning repeatedly.

A common mistake is to let a child draw you into an argument or negotiation about the punishment. Lois, whose allowance is being reduced because she forgot to take out the trash, begs for forgiveness ("I really meant to do it!"), offers a deal ("How about if I set the table *and* clear the dishes all next week?"), and tries to get a stay of execution ("Can you take half of it out of next week's allowance, and the rest out of the allowance after that?"). She may eventually wear down her parents with persistence, if not logic. Taking an early stand can end discussions like this one.

■   ■   ■   ■

When you put a new discipline system into practice, it may not function flawlessly right away. Despite excellent efforts and intentions, you and your child may slip back into old patterns. Almost inevitably, you will find yourself acting in a way that isn't consistent with your own careful planning. Take comfort in the fact that children are resilient; occasional mistakes leave no permanent damage. It's important not to get discouraged too quickly and abandon methods that are actually beginning to work.

Just as repeated episodes of disobedience and negative reactions make family life increasingly unpleasant, improved behavior gradually generates positive feelings all around. There will be less punishment and guilt, and more affection and cooperation. If you can structure a system that fosters your child's success, you will feel more successful as a parent.

PART IV

PARENTS AND PROFESSIONALS AS CO-EXPERTS

ELEVEN

DEALING WITH SCHOOL PROBLEMS

Part of your responsibility as the parent of a school-age child is to work collaboratively with educators on behalf of your son or daughter. When things are going well, this may require little more than attending routine conferences. But when there are problems, your involvement needs to be greater.

School difficulties can be frustrating for parents. You want what's best for your child, but the role you can play is limited: You're not present when the problems occur, and must rely on second-hand accounts. Other people, whose priorities are different from yours, are in charge. The most skilled and caring teacher doesn't love your child as you do; moreover, he or she must consider the needs of the entire class.

Advocating for your child doesn't require a challenging, aggressive posture. Virtually all professionals who work with children are sincerely interested in helping them, and most will welcome your input. Nor is there cause to feel intimidated, for you have much to offer: Though they have expertise on children in general, you are the expert on your particular son or daughter. This chapter shows you how to apply to school problems the techniques for understanding and communication that you have learned from this book.

CLARIFYING THE ISSUES

The evaluation approach of Part II, which is reviewed below, will help you understand what's happening and point you toward solutions.

DESCRIBE THE DIFFICULTIES

School problems fall into three broad areas: academic, behavioral, and emotional. Difficulties in any one of these domains tend to spill into the other two: A child's emotional distress may affect his behavior or learning; a youngster who gets into trouble academically could develop emotional or behavioral problems. Always keep the total picture in mind.

The first step toward understanding problems is to describe them objectively. The concepts introduced in Chapter 5 will again be useful:

- *Severity.* Is the problem mild, moderate, or severe? Imagine a spectrum, then place your child along it. For instance, disruptive behavior could range from occasional calling out to acts that bring lessons to a standstill.
- *Frequency.* How often does the behavior occur? Is it every day, or just a few times a month?
- *Duration.* How long has the problem been going on? Has the child always had the difficulty, or is it new?
- *Settings.* Does the same problem occur elsewhere—for instance, at home or in nonschool activities such as Boy Scouts?

Look at the Child

As we saw in Chapter 7, school can be the cause of a child's difficulties, or it may simply be a setting where more general emotional problems— such as depression, anxiety, poor self-image, compulsiveness, or perfectionism—are displayed. Therefore, consider:

- *Temperament.* The inborn personality traits that make a child difficult to raise also can make her hard to educate. A youngster who is intense and negatively persistent might get into frequent, loud confrontations with her teacher. A child with a low sensory threshold, who is highly sensitive to noise, may have difficulty adjusting to a large kindergarten. Understanding your child's temperament is important when you're making choices about schools or teachers, or if there are problems of fit.
- *Development.* Children usually are grouped by age in school. Therefore, a youngster whose development differs significantly from average may be subject to inappropriate expectations and have difficulties as a result. One example is the emotionally immature five-year-old who clings because she isn't ready to separate from her mother and attend kindergarten. Another is the intellectually precocious nine-year-old who misbehaves because he's bored and unchallenged by the standard fourth-grade curriculum.
- *Strengths.* A youngster's strengths can contribute to solutions. Try to think broadly: Your child may have personal assets, such as a pleasing personality. She may be kind, sensitive, and thoughtful of others. Perhaps she is bright or has specific academic talents. Or maybe she's creative, artistic, or gifted with a terrific sense of humor.

Consider Yourself and Your Family

Sometimes children have problems at school because they're reacting to something at home: A youngster could be affected by a family member's illness or by marital discord; the resulting distress might manifest itself in academic problems or misbehavior in the classroom. It's generally best to let the teacher know of such situations, so that he or she can provide extra support.

The questions below will direct your attention to aspects of family life that can affect school functioning:

- *What is your attitude toward school?* Think about your own experiences: Did you enjoy school? Were you a good student? Did you have any problems with teachers or peers?

Your educational background and beliefs might obscure your perceptions about what's good for your child. That has happened with Corey's father, who grew up hating the strict parochial schools he attended. Corey is at a small private elementary school with open classrooms, a relaxed atmosphere, and an emphasis on creativity—an environment in which his father would have thrived as a child. But Corey is a different kind of person. He's somewhat disorganized, and this relatively unstructured environment doesn't meet his needs. His teacher complains that he's inattentive in class, and his grades are poor.

Parents are not always aware of the attitudes they communicate. Sophie was a third grader who had frequent confrontations with her teacher. Her mother told me: "I admire her spunk. I had some awful teachers, but I was an absolute zero at her age, and it wouldn't have crossed my mind to question an adult." While other factors were involved in Sophie's school problems, her mother's attitude and statements also contributed.

- *Are your expectations appropriate?* Children sometimes develop school problems because of unrealistic parental expectations. One common scenario involves excessive pressure to achieve. Mothers and fathers may get caught up in the competition for admission to the "best" school or class. They become so intent on getting the child in that they ignore the far more important question: Is this the right place for *my child*? They assume that if the youngster is admitted, everything will work out. But that's not necessarily true. Pressured children can develop a wide variety of symptoms, from low self-esteem to anxiety and depression.

- *Does family life support school expectations?* What goes on at home can subtly encourage (or undermine) children's efforts regarding school. Think about school-related rules and routines in your house, such as those governing mornings and homework. Also consider your lifestyle: If your family tends to be rushed or disorganized, children may have difficulty meeting school expectations.

When Greta's sixth-grade teacher told her parents that Greta wasn't doing her homework and they carefully explored the reasons, they realized how much their own behavior had contributed. At least twice a month they kept their two daughters out of school so the family could spend a long weekend visiting relatives in another city; apparently Greta had concluded that she needn't take school obligations very seriously. Also, she shared a bedroom with her younger sister and had no quiet place to work. Her parents, whose child-rearing style encouraged early independence, never checked her assignments. When her mother and father addressed these issues, Greta's schoolwork improved.

THINK ABOUT THE SCHOOL

Most youngsters are resilient enough to adapt to a less-than-ideal classroom, teacher, or school. But for some children, a good fit is of great importance. Here are some questions to ask yourself:

- *What is the style and philosophy of the school?* What kinds of children are most appreciated there? Is it realistic to expect your child to be among them?
- *What is the classroom like?* Is it noisy or quiet? Structured or unstructured? How many children are in the class? How many boys? How many girls? Are there many very active youngsters, or others who require extra teacher attention?
- *What kind of person is the teacher?* What are her strengths and limitations? Is she an effective disciplinarian? Is she flexible or rigid? Does she yell and punish a lot?
- *Does the teacher understand and accept your child?* Does he seem to like your child? Does he favor quiet youngsters or energetic ones? Boys or girls?

COLLABORATING WITH THE TEACHER

Effective communication with the teacher is particularly important if your son or daughter runs into trouble. At such a time, the ideal relationship between you and your child's teacher is that of coexperts. To resolve the difficulties, each of you needs the support and expertise of the other. You both should feel receptive to suggestions and comfortable about offering ideas.

It's always best to approach the teacher with the assumption that he shares your desire to do what's best for your child. However, if you and the teacher feel frustrated and at a loss, accusations and defensiveness can develop. I find that breakdowns in parent-teacher communication are rarely one-sided. Consider the possibility that you might be contributing to the difficulties, and try to modify your own attitude and behavior. You and the teacher may not have compatible personalities. But you can have a positive collaboration with a teacher even in the absence of personal rapport.

The principles of the planned discussion provide an excellent basis for effective communication with your child's teacher. Here are some specific suggestions:

- *Schedule a face-to-face meeting to discuss problems.* You can't expect to make progress during hasty conversations when you're leaving your child at school or picking him up. Nor will notes or brief telephone calls suffice for any but the most minor difficulties.

Both parents should come to parent-teacher conferences if possible. This demonstrates strong family commitment. Also, having both of you there is helpful when one parent is more emotionally involved and the other is able to be more objective. Tell the teacher ahead of time that you are coming with information and questions and that you hope she will do the same. Express the desire to have a constructive exchange.

- *Prepare for the meeting.* Discuss the situation with your child to get her viewpoint. Also think about relevant characteristics of your child, any significant nonschool issues the teacher should know about, and problem-solving methods that have worked at home.

- *Maintain a neutral attitude.* Self-awareness should help—for example, in understanding how your experiences affect your perceptions and in recognizing issues of fit between you and the teacher.

- *Try to see the teacher's point of view.* You and she have different relationships with your child; you interact in different settings. Consequently, your expectations and perceptions may not be the same. Also, your child may behave differently at home and at school. This is especially true for active, excitable youngsters, who tend to do better in one-on-one situations than in a group.

Consider these statements from Miriam's mother and her first-grade teacher:

Miriam's mother: *My husband and I don't just issue orders; we explain the reasons behind them. At home, we have no problems with Miriam, so we were very surprised to hear that she's considered defiant and fresh at school. But the teacher brushed off our suggestion that she try explaining her rules to Miriam.*

Miriam's teacher: *There are twenty-eight children in my class, and several of them have special needs. There are three recent immigrants who are just learning English; I also have a hearing-impaired girl and a hyperactive boy who are being mainstreamed. I was supposed to get a part-time aide, but the budget was cut. I have to move this class through the first-grade curriculum, and it wouldn't be fair to the other children if I stopped to explain every rule to Miriam.*

INVOLVING YOUR CHILD

Any efforts to deal with a child's problems in school must include the youngster as well as the teacher and parents. Once again, planned discussions will facilitate communication. Here are some suggestions:

- *Explain the problem.* When children understand a situation, they will be more cooperative. After a conference with the teacher, parents might tell their very active eight-year-old daughter: "We know you're trying hard to behave; it's not your fault if sometimes you can't. Your teacher understands that now and she's going to help you control yourself better. She said she won't get angry so long as you try your best."

■ *Get the child's input.* It's best to talk about school problems away from the heat of a crisis. Allow the youngster to express her feelings. Ask what she thinks the problem is, and solicit her suggestions for solutions. The older she is, the more weight her views should be given.

■ *Discuss changes ahead of time.* Anything new should be explained to the child in advance. This is especially important if the change is a major one, such as a class switch, a new program or school, or a medication. In my experience, adults often assume children understand what's happening and neglect to prepare them adequately.

While you don't want to overwhelm the youngster with information, make sure he knows why the measure is being taken, how it will operate, and what he can do to help make it successful.

■   ■   ■   ■

The section below discusses the three school problems I see most frequently in my practice. I have selected situations that illustrate the full spectrum of solutions, from changes that parents can make at home, to interventions by the teacher, to special education.

SCHOOL REFUSAL

Annie, age six, had enjoyed school for the first few months. But after a combination of illness and winter vacation kept her home for three weeks, she seemed very reluctant to return. Nearly every morning, she doubled over with stomach cramps and begged to stay home. Her father, who noticed that the pain was absent on weekends, became convinced Annie was faking. When she complained about stomachaches, he brusquely told her, "Cut the performance—you're going to school no matter what!"

Annie's mother worried that their daughter might have a serious illness. She hovered over Annie and sometimes allowed her to stay home despite her father's objections. A pediatrician and a pediatric gastroenterologist examined Annie and said there was nothing physically wrong with her. The pediatrician referred her to me, and I recognized Annie as having a developing school phobia.

UNDERSTANDING THE PROBLEM

Reluctance to attend school is common. Indeed, school refusal is the leading cause of vague physical symptoms in school-age children. The problem ranges from the mild temporary reticence of a shy or immature youngster, to more persistent protests, to resistance associated with physical complaints. At the extreme end of the spectrum is **school phobia**, where the child actually becomes panicky on school mornings.

Annie's parents were right to have her physical symptoms thoroughly checked by a doctor. But once a medical cause was ruled out, it was important for everyone to adjust their thinking and look for another explanation.

- *Separation anxiety*—distress at separating from parents or home—is the most common reason for school refusal. The difficulty most often appears at the beginning of preschool, kindergarten, and first grade, and may resurface at the start of middle school or junior high. Separation difficulties are to be expected in younger children and are not a problem even in older youngsters if the reactions are brief and don't interfere significantly with functioning.

Annie was a shy child, who normally needed extra time to adjust in new situations. Her parents knew that and had made a special effort to prepare her for first grade. But they hadn't anticipated this degree of difficulty after her three-week absence from school.

- *Overprotectiveness* in a mother or father can be reflected in a youngster's separation difficulties. It's wonderful to be a loving, nurturing parent, but these healthy instincts can go too far. Sometimes parents have personal issues that cause them to keep the child too close; or they may worry too much about the dangers of the world; or they may simply get out of sync with a youngster's development, and baby her longer than necessary.

This too was a factor in Annie's situation. Her mother was a worrier. She had been a shy child herself and had been very close to her own mother; she identified with Annie and wanted to protect her as much as possible.

- *Overly high expectations for independence*—the opposite of over-protectiveness—can cause the youngster to be faced with demands he's not ready to meet. When a child strongly resists going to nursery school, his mother and father have to consider if he's really ready to go.

Parents of a late-blooming youngster should give serious thought to delaying his kindergarten entrance, especially if they're advised to do so after prekindergarten screening. With the current focus on early formal education, kindergartens have shifted from social play and experiential learning to a more academic style of instruction. As a result, some perfectly normal five-year-olds aren't ready for the intellectual or behavioral rigors of today's kindergarten.

- *Problems with the school* may be the cause of school refusal and should be suspected if there's a sudden change in a youngster who previously adjusted well. The classroom could be distressingly chaotic; maybe the child is being picked on; or possibly the academic expectations are too much for her. Or there might be problems going to and from school.

Annie's teacher could think of only a few minor problems: Annie had been disappointed when a scheduled movie was canceled, and once she had been teased by another child when she made a mistake at the blackboard. These insignificant incidents were not enough to explain the degree of Annie's distress.

SOLUTIONS

As I explained above, the youngster who balks at attending school may be sending the message, "I can't handle this!"—and there may be a real reason for this reaction. In that case, the mother and father need to address the reasons. However, if school refusal is based on separation anxiety and the child is older—as was true with Annie—the parents need to make a clear decision in their own minds that the child belongs in school, and act accordingly.

Parents often see only two alternatives: to let the child remain close, which was what Annie's mother did; or to ignore her tears and push her away, Annie's father's approach. Finding a balance is better for the youngster—and a lot easier on parents. As I told Annie's mom and dad, it's possible to give a child generous emotional support and at the same time provide the clear message that she must go to school.

Here are some recommendations I make to parents whose son or daughter resists going to school:

- *Explain any physical problems to the child.* Annie was not faking her pain, as her father suspected; however, its source was emotional and not physical. Even young children can understand a simplified explanation of how emotions affect the body. I suggested that Annie's parents tell her something like this: "You're worried about leaving home and going to school, and the worry is making your stomach muscles tighten. That's why you get a bellyache in the morning."

"What if she's really sick one day?" Annie's mother asked me. I recommended that she speak to the pediatrician and school nurse, and with their approval adopt a rule that Annie would have to go to school unless she had a temperature; if she felt ill once she got there, the school nurse could evaluate her symptoms.

- *Prepare for the unfamiliar.* A child's holding back may be partly a negative reaction to something new, rather than distress at leaving the familiar. Parents can encourage independence by helping her get acquainted with new situations and people. A shy child, like Annie, may need similar preparation before reentering a once-familiar program after time away.

- *Use structure to foster independence.* Family structure provides a supportive framework for a child who's uneasy about leaving parents: Rules and procedures eliminate decisions and arguments; routines also become comfortingly familiar.

Many parents of youngsters with school refusal are excessively involved with the child in the morning: They may dress her or pack her

schoolbag, instead of encouraging her toward appropriate independence by letting her tend to these tasks herself. I advise such parents to
help their child create a morning routine, which should be the *child's*
responsibility and not the adults'.

- *Say good-bye quickly.* Since Annie and her mother had difficulty
saying good-bye to each other, I suggested that the father temporarily
bring her to school. Her teacher, who was very helpful and concerned,
offered to greet Annie at the entrance to the building. (With a first
grader or older child, it's generally better if the parent doesn't come into
the classroom.) I advised both parents to make the moment of separation clean: Any sign of hesitation would only upset Annie.

- *Offer support and encouragement.* A young child might be com-
forted by a **transitional object**—a parent surrogate, such as a favorite
blanket or stuffed animal, that provides security. Some children like
to carry a small picture of their parents. Annie's mother sent cheerful
notes in her lunchbox. As Annie improved, her parents praised and
encouraged her, building upon her own pride in taking steps toward
independence.

- *Get professional help, if needed.* The measures above usually turn
the situation around quickly—that was the case with Annie. But if they
don't, and if a child has already missed a week of school, seek professional help right away. This is one of the few situations in which a wait-
and-see approach is not appropriate. The longer the delay, the more
likely the situation will become entrenched.

HYPERACTIVITY (ADHD)

*Henry was a very active eight-year-old whose family moved just before he
entered third grade. During September, his teacher called his parents to
express concern about his wild behavior. They explained that Henry had
found the move stressful and promised, "He'll settle down soon." However,
the situation deteriorated instead of getting better.*

*The teacher complained that Henry was inattentive and disruptive.
She said, "He never listens to me." He often left his seat without permission*

or talked out of turn. When the group was taken through the halls to the gym or cafeteria, Henry sometimes ran off and wandered into other classrooms. His parents saw similar inattention and impulsive behavior at home, but didn't find it as troubling. They came to me for the first time after the teacher insisted that Henry be tested for hyperactivity.

UNDERSTANDING ADHD

A child's activity level can range from placid to very active. To me, "hyperactive" is simply an adjective that describes an unusually high level of activity. But the term is popularly used as synonymous with a syndrome called "attention-deficit/hyperactivity disorder" (ADHD), a psychiatric diagnosis describing extremely high activity and impulsivity, or marked inattention—or a combination of these traits. I believe that too many children receive a clinical diagnosis of ADHD; I reserve this term for the youngster who is so active, impulsive, and distractible that he or she would have difficulty functioning in nearly any setting. And indeed, many professionals are becoming more conservative about making this diagnosis.

Many children can become wild at times. At any particular moment, a youngster's activity level is affected by many factors, including his temperament, maturity, diet, medication, and environment. Henry was much more active than average, but his parents usually were able to prevent him from getting into mischief at home. At school, where the level of stimulation was much higher, there were problems.

There is some evidence that biological factors are involved in determining a child's activity level. Genetic factors, biochemical deficits, and differences in brain structure have been postulated as playing a role in ADHD.

Some of these children have associated problems in the areas of learning, language development, and physical coordination. They're often temperamentally difficult in other ways, with high intensity and poor adaptability, which make transitions difficult. They tend to be stubborn and unpredictable. At the same time, they're usually sunny and cheerful, and forward-going rather than shy. They may be talented in music, athletics, or other areas. They're often empathetic and intuitive. Their strengths and talents should never be forgotten.

An ADHD diagnosis usually is made by a child psychiatrist, pediatric neurologist, psychologist, or behaviorally oriented pediatrician, based on observation, parent and teacher reports, and the child's history. It's important to remember that there are no definitive physical tests that pinpoint ADHD—no blood markers of chemical imbalance, abnormal brain waves, or specific indicators on an X-ray. All so-called "tests" for hyperactivity are simply rating scales or checklists of behavior and are open to subjective interpretation. If two teachers use the same checklist to rate a youngster, the results might be considerably different: Squirming or interrupting that one considers excessive could look normal to the other.

While rating scales are useful for organizing impressions and describing behavior more objectively, they create an illusion of precision. This may lead parents and professionals to think of hyperactivity as a medical illness with a specific drug cure.

SOLUTIONS

When a child's activity level leads to behavior problems, solutions cover a range from better planning and structure to improved fit, to a change in school or class, to professional help, which may include individual or group therapy, behavioral approaches, medication, or special education.

▪ *Improved fit and better management.* These are always helpful and often all that's needed. At my suggestion, Henry's parents scheduled a conference with his teacher. Though they felt that her view of their son was too negative, they resolved to take a positive approach. They prepared for the meeting by listing ideas they had found helpful. Here's how the conference went, according to their description:

> TEACHER: *I really like Henry, but he needs a lot of supervision,*
> *and I can't always provide that.*
> MOTHER: *We know Henry can be a handful, and I can imag-*

ine that's difficult when you are responsible for a whole class-room. At home, we've noticed patterns to his behavior, and that's been a big help. Are there any occasions when problems come up a lot?

TEACHER: *Well, the worst time is in the morning. He's usually a little late, and it takes him a long time to settle down.*

MOTHER: *Uh-oh, that's our fault! My husband and I work, and mornings tend to be pretty hectic.*

FATHER: *We've been talking about setting the alarm fifteen minutes earlier, so we wouldn't be so rushed.*

TEACHER: *Anything that made Henry calmer in the morning would be helpful.*

MOTHER: *I appreciate the suggestion. This is something we've been meaning to address.*

TEACHER: *There are also problems in the hallway, going to and from the gym or the cafeteria. He sometimes disturbs other classes.*

FATHER: *Would it be possible for him to walk with you? Going shopping used to be difficult, but now we have a rule that he has to hold hands with one of us, and it makes a big difference.*

TEACHER: *I'll try that—it might very well help. But I can't hold his hand in class or in the lunch line.*

FATHER: *Could he get his lunch a few minutes early, so he wouldn't have to stand on line?*

TEACHER: *No, he would have to be brought to the cafeteria by a staff member, and there's no one available. What about giving him a bag lunch?*

MOTHER: *That's a good idea—we'll do it.*

TEACHER: *It's very hard for me to get him to obey instructions.*

MOTHER: *Sometimes with Henry the problem isn't deliberately disobeying, but forgetting or not paying attention.*

TEACHER: *Well, it comes down to the same thing.*

MOTHER: *I find that if I catch his eye before I tell him something, he's more likely to hear it.*

TEACHER: *Good idea. I think I'll also change his seat. He sits in the back now, and I'll move him closer to me.*

FATHER: *We've noticed that after he's been sitting for a while, he gets very restless. When we see him swinging his legs, we know he needs a break. Might it be possible for him to get up and do something useful every once in a while? Could he run an errand for you?*

TEACHER: *I don't think he's ready to be out in the halls by himself. But I'll try to give him breaks more often in the classroom. He's always eager to be helpful.*

FATHER: *I think these changes will make a difference—they certainly have at home. We'll explain to Henry that you're trying to help him behave better.*

TEACHER: *I'll speak to him as well. You know, I feel optimistic that things will improve.*

The teacher changed Henry's seat and began keeping him next to her when the group left the classroom. Though the problems did not disappear entirely, his behavior improved considerably as a result of these and other changes by the teacher and at home.

Later in the year, however, a series of unfortunate circumstances coincided to create a crisis: Henry's regular teacher became seriously ill, and an inexperienced substitute took over the class. In addition, several disruptions at home altered the family's new morning routine and made his parents less available. Henry's behavior deteriorated during this period. One day, when a water leak kept the class confined to their room during lunch and recess, Henry ran out of the classroom and led the substitute teacher on a chase through the building. Before she caught up with him in the school library, he had knocked over and ruined a display of student artwork. The substitute angrily called Henry's parents and asked them to come to school for a conference the next day. Clearly, new measures were needed.

■ *A respite.* If the problems are of crisis proportions, everyone—child, parents, and teacher—may be temporarily unable to work toward long-term objectives. In such situations, I often recommend that parents keep the child out of school for a couple of days. The respite gives everyone a chance to calm down; it also interrupts the behavior patterns that caused the problems. Afterward, the school and family are far more able to find more lasting solutions. Henry's parents, with the consent of the substitute teacher and school principal, did this. They also returned to see me.

■ *Changing to another class or school.* When less extensive measures aren't enough, and the fit is very poor, a more substantial change in the child's environment must be considered. Switching to another class is one possibility. A different teacher might provide more structure—or more flexibility, if that's what your child needs. A very active, easily excited youngster might do better in a smaller class, where there's increased supervision and reduced stimulation.

Changing schools is another option. That doesn't necessarily mean private school. A child might be able to attend public school in another district; there may be a magnet or experimental school that provides extra services.

Henry's parents decided to investigate a private school in their community that had an excellent reputation. They asked me how frank they should be in discussing his problems with the headmaster there. Understandably, they didn't want to jeopardize his chances of being accepted. I told them, "If you want a new environment that will meet Henry's needs, you have to let the school know what kind of child this is. It may be painful if they say they can't deal with him, but that's much better than having to face trouble later on."

■ *Therapy.* Both a hyperactive child and his parents may benefit from help. Parent guidance aimed at improving management and fit is always part of the treatment when I work with such a youngster. I also may offer individual therapy to address self-image issues: Understandably, a child who is unable to keep himself from getting into trouble can develop self-image problems. Certain behavioral techniques can help an impulsive youngster slow himself down; Chapter 12 describes some of these methods.

■ *Medication.* Though the above measures are always helpful, they may not be enough to make the behavior of a hyperactive, impulsive, and distractible child acceptable in school. In such a case, medication should be considered as well. Ritalin (methylphenidate) is the drug most commonly prescribed for hyperactivity, but others also are effective; they can be tried if a child doesn't respond to Ritalin.

Parents may be very distressed at the prospect of having their child take medication for hyperactivity, and indeed there is some reason for concern. Though Ritalin is generally safe, it can have unpleasant side effects, such as headache, stomachache, listlessness, sleep and appetite disturbances, and emotional upset; these usually are temporary. There is controversy about using it with a child who has tics or a family history of tics. Children who take Ritalin for protracted periods may grow more slowly, though they catch up once they're off the drug. (The earlier fear that Ritalin could lead to later drug abuse has proven unfounded.)

Critics correctly point out that drugs are overprescribed for hyperactivity, often not monitored adequately, and sometimes used as a quick and easy solution instead of making desirable improvements in the child's environment. Overprescription can be a byproduct of inappropriate medical thinking: seeing hyperactivity as an illness and Ritalin as the cure.

While these points are valid, ideal alternatives aren't always available, and parents may have to choose among imperfect options. Medication has benefits as well as drawbacks. Ritalin and other drugs used for hyperactivity increase attention span and decrease disruptive behavior. Between 60 and 90 percent of children who take these drugs improve substantially: They become less impulsive and restless, and more attentive and accurate in their schoolwork. Sometimes the change means that a youngster can remain in a regular classroom instead of switching into a special-education program.

I believe that medication should be viewed as one potential strategy in a more comprehensive plan for helping the child; it should never be the only measure taken. I prescribe Ritalin when efforts to improve fit and management are not adequate, and the youngster continues to suffer because he cannot meet expectations at school. I also use it to provide temporary relief in a crisis, when everyone is too upset to implement better management.

I generally start with a small amount and increase the dose gradually, based on the child's response. Once the youngster is doing better, and improved management methods are in place, I usually suggest that the medication be reduced or discontinued on a trial basis.

This recommendation sometimes alarms parents who have seen a welcome improvement because of Ritalin. I remind them of two things: First, Ritalin is a short-acting medication. That means you see results quickly and can readily adjust. If you stop it on a trial basis and there are problems, going back on the medication will produce an effect right away. Second, and more important, medication is only one reason that the child has changed; new family patterns and school changes also deserve credit, and they will continue to operate.

Henry's regular teacher returned to school about the same time he did, and things settled down for the rest of the term. The following year the class was larger, the teacher was less responsive, and there were problems almost immediately.

Henry's mother took a week off from work to explore other schools and programs. The private school they had investigated earlier had no openings, and despite extensive efforts, the parents could find no promising alternatives. Faced with a worsening situation, the parents decided to try Ritalin.

Henry responded well to medication: His behavior improved immediately, and there were no side effects. I suggested that he see a behavioral therapist to learn self-control techniques; this too was successful. A few months later, I reduced Henry's dose of Ritalin; he remained on a low dose through fourth grade, and there were no further problems. That summer he went off the medication. His parents called the following fall to say that Henry was doing well in fifth grade.

LEARNING DISABILITIES

Doug, age eleven, was carrying an enormous schoolbag when he came to my office for the first time. His sad expression suggested that texts and notebooks were not the only burden he bore. Doug's parents were deeply concerned about his unhappiness. They told me that he had become listless and withdrawn and had lost his passion for playing basketball with his friends.

Doug had been tested for learning disabilities in second grade: Although he clearly was very bright, he hadn't yet learned to read. Since then, he had received assistance from the school's resource room, supplemented by private tutoring, therapy, and special weekend classes arranged by his parents. Over the years, these measures had expanded considerably. By the time I saw Doug, he was a sixth grader, and his weekly schedule was as crowded as that of any busy executive.

Doug was about to graduate from elementary school. His guidance counselor and the school's learning-disabilities specialist had strongly recommended that he attend a special-education program next year, rather than the regular junior high. Doug's parents were very reluctant to consider this possibility. "We believe that mainstreaming is best," they told me.

UNDERSTANDING LEARNING DISABILITIES

There are many reasons that a child has difficulty learning. It may have to do with the teacher, the class composition, anxiety or depression, or the youngster's level of intelligence. The term "learning disability" generally implies that the child has at least a normal IQ but that her "mental wiring" doesn't function the way it does in most children. This makes it harder for her to learn through conventional teaching methods.

As with most difficulties, neurologically based learning problems fall along a spectrum. At the mild end of the range is a **developmental lag:** A child has temporarily fallen behind his peers and will catch up, perhaps needing minimal help to do so. Farther out along the spectrum is a **learning difference:** The youngster has an unusual learning style. Maybe listening doesn't suffice, and he needs lessons with a strong visual component; or perhaps he's able to learn global concepts, but has difficulty following details. If these differences are great enough, and the child has trouble functioning in the classroom, the problem may be called a **learning dysfunction** or, in extreme cases, a **learning disability**.

There's no universally accepted point at which a learning problem is classified as a learning disability—different school systems and different professionals apply different standards. I believe that the term "learning disability" should be reserved for the far end of the spectrum. Too many average children, whose parents and teachers expect them to perform at above-average levels, are being identified as learning disabled. This was not the case with Doug, however: He had a true learning disability.

Professional assessment of learning problems may be undertaken at the request of the parents or the teacher. Testing can be useful: An objective evaluation can clarify a situation by describing a child's abilities and weaknesses. Ideally, this will enable the school staff to devise an individualized plan to help the child.

Unfortunately, testing for learning disabilities sometimes goes too far. Instead of producing a practical educational plan, the tests can generate voluminous reports that merely add to the confusion. I believe that briefer initial assessments often are more appropriate and that extensive investigations should be made more selectively. If children were screened with inexpensive, rapid tests, and simple measures were implemented for those with relatively minor problems, many more youngsters could be helped.

Solutions

When a child isn't learning well, the spectrum of solutions ranges from minor adjustments by the teacher to placement in a separate special-education program. Obviously, any correctable learning problem should be addressed. But I believe that the central goal of intervention should be to support the child's strengths and to help him find ways around his weaknesses.

▪ *Compensation in the classroom.* A flexible, creative teacher can devise ways for a youngster to compensate for learning problems, such as allowing him to take extra time on tests or to present a report orally rather than in writing. The school may offer special services—such as tutoring, counseling, or occupational or language therapy—that give the child extra help for part of the day while he spends the rest of his time in a regular class.

▪ *Extra family support.* Parents can assist the child with homework or provide a tutor; the simpler the problems, the less expert the assistance needs to be. Even more important, parents can find ways to bolster the strengths of a youngster for whom learning is difficult.

- *Special education.* Federal legislation guarantees a "free appropriate education" for all children with disabilities. In general, a youngster must be diagnosed as having a learning, emotional, behavioral, or physical handicap before he can receive special-education services. Such youngsters receive an individual educational plan (IEP) designed to meet their needs. (If your child has a learning disability, ask the school guidance counselor or principal where to get information about your legal rights; also locate parent support groups, which can be very helpful.)

It's unfortunate that most public education systems don't offer smaller classes for normal or mildly impaired children who need more individual attention than can be given in a large class. Also unfortunate is the insistence that youngsters receive a diagnosis before they can get services. I encourage parents to think of the label as an administrative requirement and not an indictment of their child.

Doug's parents and I discussed the pros and cons of his attending a special-education school, rather than being mainstreamed:

FATHER: *My son is no dummy, but go tell that to the kids in the neighborhood. He'll be stuck with that label, and his self-image—which isn't so hot anyway—will fall apart. And I worry about the future: What decent college will accept him from that kind of school? It's not as if he's failing his courses.*

ST: *Believe me, I understand your concerns; I agree that mainstreaming is best whenever possible. But it's my experience that children suffer far less from placement in a good special school than from remaining in a situation where they're continually struggling. Your son's passing grades are remarkable considering his disabilities, and that's a credit to the support he's gotten from you and his school. But look at the heavy price he's paying: His schedule is exhausting; he's clearly unhappy; and, as you say, his self-image is not so hot.*

MOTHER: *The school they're suggesting sounds all wrong for*

Doug: It's called the Deerhaven School for Handicapped Children.

ST: *The name certainly is unfortunate, but as you know, the term "handicapped" has become a catch-all. Ignore the name, and check out the program. Look at the children and the teachers; observe the activities. Focus on the most important questions: Is this a school environment that would meet Doug's needs? Could he be successful there? And ask the same questions about the junior high school.*

FATHER: *His academic needs are being met fairly well right now.*

ST: *Is "fairly well" what you really want for Doug?*

Doug's parents agreed to visit the recommended school with their son and were greatly reassured by what they saw. He's now attending the school and is happy there, his parents report.

■   ■   ■   ■

The fact that your child is having problems in school should not leave you with a sense of helplessness. As you've seen in this chapter, you can be a strong advocate for your child. The power you bring to this role rests mainly upon the understanding and knowledge you offer. You will be most effective if you approach the school with a positive, cooperative attitude, prepared to join sensible efforts on the child's behalf. Try to involve your child whenever possible, and always remain aware of his strengths and talents.

TWELVE

SEEKING PROFESSIONAL HELP

Many mild-to-moderate problems melt away when parents apply the principles of planned communication, acceptance, and discipline. I hope that what you've learned up to this point has enabled you to improve your child's situation, and that no further help is needed. However, in some instances, professional involvement is necessary as well. This may have been clear from the beginning; or perhaps it became evident as you read the book, adopted the recommended measures, and found they weren't enough.

Acknowledging that your child needs outside help doesn't mean you have failed as a parent, or that there's nothing more you can do. **Professional and self-help are complementary, not mutually exclusive.** If you've performed the evaluation in Chapters 5 through 7, you have information that will greatly enhance your collaboration with a professional.

"Getting professional help" could mean taking your child to a psychotherapist, but not necessarily. Other possibilities include consulting a behaviorally oriented doctor or a nutritionist; also, there are valuable forms of nonprofessional assistance to consider, such as parent support groups. Though this chapter is concerned primarily with mental-health professionals, I encourage you to be open to other options too.

REASONS TO SEE A MENTAL-HEALTH PROFESSIONAL

There are three reasons to seek help from a mental-health professional: You're faced with an emergency; the problems are severe and extensive; or your own efforts haven't been fully successful. When you're not sure, it's best to err on the side of caution and get expert advice.

REASON 1: EMERGENCIES

Sometimes a problem begins so suddenly, or is so severe, that immediate professional attention is required. Here are signs that your child needs help right away:

- *Bizarre behavior.* Examples are a child hearing voices, seeing things that aren't there, or insisting that he can fly.
- *Severe anxiety reactions.* The child becomes panicky and can't be calmed. One example is the youngster who is so terrified by the prospect of going to school that she cries uncontrollably.
- *Dangerous behavior.* The youngster's acts threaten others or himself. Examples are setting a fire, hurting an animal, assaulting a classmate, or running away from home.
- *Suicidal behavior.* This includes suicide attempts, talking about suicide, or making specific suicide plans.

In an emergency, call your child's therapist (if he has one), his pediatrician, or the family doctor. Or take the youngster to a hospital emergency room. If there's a good children's hospital near you, that's best; if not, go to a reputable psychiatric hospital or general hospital.

REASON 2: THE PROBLEMS ARE EXTENSIVE

The more complicated your child's difficulties, and the more troubled your family situation, the more important it is to seek help early. This is not to say that you won't be able to make positive changes on your own. But complex, severe, long-standing problems also need professional attention.

Jeffrey is a vulnerable youngster with learning disabilities who recently changed schools. He is anxious and unhappy and struggling both academically and socially. Jeffrey's mother suffers from chronic fatigue syndrome and has limited energy; his father is depressed. This is a complicated situation in which all family members are troubled. Help for them might include individual therapy for Jeffrey, antidepressant medication for his father, and a support group for his mother, who is already under medical care.

Perhaps you know what needs to be done but simply can't summon the necessary time and energy. You might be under pressure to perform at work and anxious about your future. Or maybe you're caring for an invalid mother or father on top of your parental obligations. You could be depressed yourself or struggling to overcome drug or alcohol dependence. In the meantime, your child is experiencing increasing difficulty. Under such circumstances, the guidance of a mental-health professional would benefit you and your child.

REASON 3: PARENTAL CHANGES AREN'T ENOUGH

You may accomplish a great deal on your own but find that more is needed. A professional can help you build upon your initial success. I'm sometimes consulted by parents who have read my first book, *The Difficult Child*. Typically, the youngster has improved somewhat with better management. Though the parents are gratified by the positive changes, they realize that more could be done.

FINDING THE RIGHT THERAPIST

Once you've determined that help is needed, your next step is to find an appropriate therapist. While you want your child to be seen by a well-qualified individual, you needn't spend months searching for the ideal person. Rarely does a youngster need the assistance of a renowned authority.

TYPES OF MENTAL-HEALTH PROFESSIONALS

The terms "mental-health professional" and "therapist" encompass individuals with a wide range of training and experience. In my specialty, psychiatry, therapists are M.D.s, licensed to practice medicine and to prescribe drugs, who have completed a psychiatric residency. In addition, some obtain board certification in psychiatry by taking rigorous examinations given by the American Board of Psychiatry and Neurology; additional training and testing is required for qualification and board certification in child psychiatry.

A therapist who isn't a psychiatrist could have a background in psychology, social work, nursing, education, or religion. Some identify themselves by their education, training, or license. Others refer to their area of special interest: Examples are marriage or family therapists, cognitive or behavior therapists, and parent counselors. "Eclectic" therapists consider themselves competent in several forms of treatment.

Some therapists are in private practice; others work in clinics that may be independent or affiliated with a hospital, university, or other institution. Mental-health clinics may cover all problems, or they might specialize in particular issues (for example stress, phobias or eating disorders); they may offer many forms of treatment, or just one. In general, clinics provide more options than private therapists; their fees may be lower or on a sliding scale. However, you could be assigned to a therapist rather than selecting one yourself; also, there may be rotation of staff during the course of treatment.

WHAT KIND OF THERAPIST IS NEEDED?

Sometimes the answer will be obvious. If a formerly independent six-year-old girl becomes clingy when her parents develop marital problems, they would look for a therapist who can help them as well as their child. A hyperactive seven-year-old boy whose school difficulties have continued despite placement in a special class probably needs medication and should be seen by a child psychiatrist.

Other situations are less clear. Though Alyssa is only eleven, her heavy makeup and seductive clothing make her look more like a sixteen-year-old. She spends most of her time hanging around the local high school with a group of rebellious older children, and she has stopped doing homework. There are also family problems: Her father, a pharmacist, just entered treatment for drug dependence, and there are significant marital tensions.

Alyssa's parents have received conflicting advice from her teachers and their friends. Some say this is simply early adolescent rebelliousness that should be nipped in the bud with strict limits; others see her behavior as a symptom of deeper problems and recommend therapy. Alyssa's parents are convinced that their own difficulties are to blame. They want to take action, but don't know where to start. In a complex situation like this one, their first step should be an evaluation by a broadly trained, experienced professional who can help them sort things out and recommend an appropriate course of treatment.

Under certain circumstances, you might need to consult a respected authority, such as the chairman of the child psychiatry department at a teaching hospital, or a recognized expert on a particular subject. The need for such a consultation would arise if other professionals give you widely differing opinions about the best course of action to pursue. Or you might want a second opinion if your child is already in therapy and it doesn't seem to be working. I sometimes provide such expertise when difficult temperament may be a factor in a child's problems.

GETTING A REFERRAL

Usually, the best way to find a therapist is through a personal referral. One source is your child's pediatrician or the family doctor. The school psychologist, social worker, guidance counselor, and other staff members also can be consulted, especially if school problems are involved. When teacher cooperation is required for treatment, it's very helpful to have a therapist who already has good relationships with the staff.

You might seek a recommendation from a member of the clergy, a nurse—or anyone who sees many families with problems. Relevant support groups often are excellent referral resources. One of the best ways to find a therapist is to follow the recommendation of another parent whose child has been successfully treated for a similar difficulty.

Regardless of the source, ask why a particular person is being suggested. Is this someone with special expertise? Has he or she been helpful in a situation like yours? Or is the therapist simply a friend of the person whom you asked for a referral?

Less personal, but sometimes helpful, are community resources and publications. You can call the psychiatry or psychology department of a hospital—preferably a children's hospital. Local chapters of national professional organizations usually make referrals to their members. Examples include the American Academy of Child and Adolescent Psychiatry, the American Psychiatric Association, the American Psychological Association, and the National Association of Social Workers. Some communities publish resource guides that list mental-health professionals—ask at your local library or bookstore.

What if options are restricted by your insurance company, HMO, or by family finances? Discuss the problem frankly with your referral source, insurance company, or therapist. Sometimes rules can be bent; less costly alternatives may be available.

OBTAINING PRELIMINARY INFORMATION

To help you decide (or to prepare you for your first appointment once you've made a choice), get basic information about the therapist. Some practices routinely provide information sheets or brochures; otherwise, speak with the therapist or an assistant. Here are questions to ask:

- *What is your background?* Most of the time, the specifics of an individual's training and affiliations are less important than his experience and reputation. However, you should make sure the therapist is licensed—that means he has met at least minimal standards of training and experience.
- *What kinds of patients do you usually treat?* This is important if your child's or family's circumstances are unusual in a way relevant to treatment. Perhaps the youngster has suffered a particular trauma, such as incest; or she may have a relatively rare physical condition, like blindness or a facial deformity, that raises special issues. Or your family's religious beliefs may limit the changes you can make. Ask the therapist about her experience with youngsters like yours. It's best to consult someone who sees similar children regularly, not just once every few years.
- *What is your procedure with new clients?* Find out which family members should come to the first appointment. Ask how long the initial evaluation will take, what it will consist of, and when you will hear the therapist's recommendations.
- *What are your fees?* Don't hesitate to raise financial questions. You may want to check with your insurance company about coverage before the first visit.

PREPARING YOURSELF AND YOUR CHILD

Some parents find it painful to acknowledge the need for help. Anticipating their first contact with the therapist, they may feel anxious, guilty, or ambivalent. They may expect to be scrutinized and criticized. If the suggestion to seek advice came from someone else—a member of the school staff, perhaps—they may feel defensive.

When parents seem uncomfortable about consulting me, or worried about the impact that seeing a psychiatrist might have on their child, I suggest they think of the first visit as an evaluation, where the intent is simply to clarify the situation. I remind them that an initial consultation does not commit them to further treatment. Obviously, I will need to observe the family and their interactions, and I must ask the probing questions required for a full history. But I make every effort to be neutral and respectful. Trying to understand a family does not mean that I'm sitting in judgment and waiting to pounce on them.

Children are not harmed by a properly conducted interview with a mental-health professional, but some preparation is advisable. Explain to the child that she is about to see a helpful person. You might say something like: "Ms. Jones helps families get along better" or "Dr. Smith helps children who are afraid to go to sleep." I advise parents to reassure young children that I'm not the kind of doctor who gives injections. If the child is older and embarrassed at the prospect of seeing me, the parent could say: "Going to a psychiatrist doesn't mean you're crazy. Lots of normal kids have problems."

THE FIRST SESSION

Your initial contact with the therapist lets her make a preliminary assessment of your child's situation—and also allows you to decide if she is right for your family. Some mental-health professionals begin by interviewing the family together; others start with the parents or the child. I generally see both parents and the child on a first visit.

A history—at a minimum covering the child's current and past problems, and the family and school environment—should be taken at these initial sessions. You (and the child's teacher if there are problems in school) might be asked to fill out questionnaires about the youngster's background and behavior.

You may wonder what goes on when the child is interviewed alone. During the first session, most therapists try to establish rapport, as well as to elicit information. They might begin by asking general questions such as, "How old are you?" and "Where do you go to school?"

Gradually, the discussion will turn to the child's feelings about his situation, his relationships, and himself.

Another purpose of the initial visit is for you to form an impression of the therapist, personally and professionally. Mental-health professionals are human; they have different personalities and backgrounds. You want someone with whom you and your child feel comfortable and able to communicate.

You will learn something from her office and routines. A person who treats children should have a child-friendly office and waiting room. Consideration of parents (or lack of it) is also revealing.

At the end of the initial assessment, expect the therapist to share her impressions and recommendations. These should make sense to you. Don't hesitate to ask questions. A good professional should welcome them and respond frankly. If the therapist describes an approach whose rationale you don't understand, ask "Why?" The answer should reflect a rational decision based on your situation.

If therapy is recommended for your child, find out what role the therapist expects you to play during treatment. The younger your son or daughter, the more involved you should be. There are situations in which it is important for the therapist to have an individual, confidential relationship with your child. The older the youngster, the more likely that this will be true. The legitimate need to protect the private relationship with a patient doesn't mean that therapy takes place in an ivory tower, however. Parents are entitled to have general feedback about the progress of treatment, and dangerous behavior should never be kept confidential. A therapist should be willing to collaborate with you and with your child's school, physician, and any other professionals working on his behalf.

FORMS OF TREATMENT

Some parents are concerned that therapy will inevitably be an open-ended, expensive process. Indeed, long-term individual therapy once was virtually the only form of treatment practiced. This is no longer the case. A wide range of options is available today, and many modern approaches are brief and practical.

The descriptions below are meant to give you a sense of the possibilities, rather than to cover every type of therapy or to convey what specific psychotherapists actually do. Sometimes more than one professional is needed for optimal treatment. A child might have individual therapy with a psychologist and attend group-therapy sessions to work on social skills. She might be under the care of a psychiatrist or other physician to receive medication and see a behavioral psychologist to learn relaxation techniques. Good therapists know their limits and will refer you to someone else if your child needs help they cannot provide.

While some therapists use only one type of treatment, such as play therapy or behavior therapy, most experienced professionals use several techniques. In general, the goals are to instill hope and improved morale; promote realistic self-acceptance; work on mastery and coping; and change maladaptive patterns of behavior. A good relationship with the therapist is always important.

Here are some of the most widely used treatment approaches:

PSYCHODYNAMICALLY-ORIENTED LONG-TERM THERAPY

This is an intensive treatment method that may be suitable for a child whose inner conflicts contribute significantly to his problems. A youngster might see the therapist once or twice weekly for a year or more. (Psychoanalysis, an even more extensive and lengthy process, rarely is used with children.)

Cara, age ten, comes from an achievement-oriented family. Her older brother died when she was five. Though Cara is bright and hardworking, she is also extremely demanding of herself. Over the years she has developed an internal system of self-criticism that leaves her depressed and frustrated in the face of anything short of perfection. Her unreasonably high standards are interfering with her school performance and, more generally, with her enjoyment of life. Because so much rides on anything she undertakes, she procrastinates, doesn't try hard, and sometimes seems to fail deliberately.

In individual therapy, I would explore Cara's guilt, her unconscious need to compensate her parents for the loss of their son—and the rage she feels about being the model child, which is being expressed inwardly through her self-criticism and failure. The goal of treatment would be to help Cara resolve this conflict and achieve comfortable self-acceptance.

BRIEF THERAPY

This form of treatment, as the name implies, is usually time-limited. Goals are specific; the therapist takes an active role. Brief therapy generally is undertaken for problems of recent onset in otherwise well-adjusted children—for example, a youngster who has experienced some traumatic incident, such as a single episode of sexual abuse or a hospitalization. The therapist provides a supportive environment and helps the youngster ventilate feelings through talk or play.

Sometimes brief therapy, with a termination date set at the outset, is used with children who have suffered a loss, such as the death of a parent. The planned ending of the relationship between the child and therapist is itself a feature of the treatment, since it replicates the experience of loss, but in a healthier way.

SUPPORTIVE THERAPY

This method is used with children facing severe family problems, or with youngsters too fragile to tolerate more exploratory approaches. The child's relationship with the therapist is of prime importance.

June, age twelve, is the oldest of four children and has the domestic responsibilities of an adult. Her father abandoned the family several years ago; since then her mother has become increasingly promiscuous and irresponsible. June uses denial to cope: On days when her mother keeps her home from school to take care of her baby brother, she claims, "My mom thinks I'm coming down with a cold." She is seen regularly by the social worker at her junior high school. At this point, the primary purpose of therapy is to give June a stable, supportive relationship with an adult.

PLAY THERAPY

This technique is used for communicating with young children. Instead of talking about himself, his feelings, or people he knows, the child tells stories or plays with dolls, puppets, or games; often these are specially designed for therapeutic use. The younger the child, the more likely the therapist is to use play.

Brittany, age five, was brought to me because she was unhappy, having trouble with peers, and increasingly resisted going to school. The difficulties had started with her bossy behavior; other children had reacted with teasing—and both had escalated.

Since Brittany denied she had any problems and claimed she had "lots of friends," I approached her with doll play. I started a story about a doll who was afraid to go to school and asked Brittany to tell me what happened next. Gradually, her feelings emerged.

COGNITIVE THERAPY

Treatment is based on the assumption that problems can be addressed by correcting faulty thinking. It is often incorporated into other forms of therapy.

I use a cognitive approach when it seems advisable to recruit the child's logic and willpower. That was the case with Ethan, an eight-year-old boy whose father consulted me because he seemed very angry at his stepmother. When I talked with Ethan, it became clear that his stepmother was not the source of the problem. Like many children of divorced parents, Ethan longed for his mother and father to reunite. He had developed the magical belief that if he ignored his father's remarriage, the wished-for reunion would occur.

During my sessions with Ethan, I first allowed him to express his feelings. Next, the cognitive component of therapy focused on the lack of logic in his actions:

> ST: *You came home, your stepmother said "Hello" to you, and you ignored her. What did you hope would happen?*

ETHAN: *I don't know—I just want her to leave. I want everything to be the way it was before she came. It was way better then.*

ST: *Your dad and your stepmother are married. When I talked to them, they told me that they love each other very much. You know that. So it doesn't make sense to hope that your stepmother is going to leave.*

ETHAN: *I don't care. That's what I want.*

ST: *Well, what happened after your stepmother said "Hello" and you ignored her?*

ETHAN: *My dad got mad at me. He gave me this boring lecture and sent me to my room. He always takes her side.*

ST: *So look what happened: You were trying to make your stepmother leave, and instead you got punished. Where's the sense of that?*

Through this and similar discussions, Ethan eventually accepted the fact that his fantasy would not become real. At a follow-up visit six months later, his father told me that his son's behavior toward his stepmother was now acceptable.

BEHAVIOR THERAPY

This approach is based on the view that many problems are simply bad habits resulting from faulty learning and that other learning can correct these patterns. Treatment usually involves systematic assessments of behavior and the shaping of better responses.

I'm impressed by how useful certain behavioral techniques can be with children, and I have incorporated some of them in my practice. But when a youngster needs more behavioral help than I can provide, I refer the family to a specialist. For example, Barry, a very tense and fearful nine-year-old, couldn't master any of the relaxation techniques I attempted to teach him. But when he was trained at a stress clinic by a behavioral psychologist who used biofeedback, and he could see the relationship between his efforts and such physical responses as heart rate and perspiration, his symptoms improved.

Parents and teachers often use behavioral methods without labeling them as such. Indeed, much of the advice in self-help books and parent-education programs is behavioral in emphasis. More specialized books and tapes are available in bookstores or libraries if you're interested in pursuing on your own any of the behavioral approaches mentioned below. Because behavioral techniques require the active cooperation of the child, it's especially important that the youngster understand what's being done and why. Here are some common approaches:

- *Relaxation techniques* can be helpful with fears, anxiety, worries, sleep and separation problems, and physical tension. Be aware, though, that learning them requires a commitment on your part, even if your child works with a therapist: They are most effective when you help him practice. Ideally, he eventually will learn to apply the techniques on his own, so that he can manage his problems himself.

Deep breathing—slowly and rhythmically inhaling and exhaling—is simple enough for a therapist or parent to teach even a very young child. An imaginative youngster might benefit from **visualization**, in which the adult guides her (and later she guides herself) to imagine a peaceful scene where she feels comfortable. This can be very useful at times of tension or to combat fears. **Progressive muscular relaxation**—alternately tensing and relaxing the major muscles, starting with the feet and moving up to the head—is helpful when youngsters are too tense to fall asleep.

- *Techniques for countering fears* work for general anxiety as well as for specific fears. Any of the relaxation methods described above can be useful too.

Some youngsters are subject to frightening thoughts that make them unable to fall asleep. They may benefit from **thought substitution:** The child is directed to substitute some specific pleasant fantasy—which must be practiced in advance—for the fearsome thought. For example, I suggested thought substitution for a ten-year-old boy who was having recurring fears of being killed by a robber while he slept. At my direction, he went over the fantasy in detail and decided that at the moment the killer was about to strike, he would substitute the thought of himself getting the winning goal in a soccer game. After a few days of practice, he was able to banish his fear.

Self-talk can be used to counter fears of separation and of new or intimidating situations. The child is taught to repeat specific encouragements. A youngster who is afraid of walking to school alone might tell herself: "I'm six and I'm a brave girl."

Because young children are much more suggestible than adults, they often respond well to **positive magical thinking**. Monsters may disappear with applications of "monster spray"; a **brave companion** (simply any stuffed animal so designated) can help a frightened child feel courageous.

Finally, specific fears may be countered by **systematic desensitization**—exposing a child gradually to a feared object. This is particularly effective when an otherwise emotionally sturdy youngster develops a fear of animals, such as dogs. By starting with something innocuous like a toy dog, and moving up to dogs seen from afar on the street, a child may eventually overcome her fright and be able to pet a real dog.

- *Techniques for changing behavior* can counter general impulsivity or specific bad habits. Teaching impulsive youngsters to **stop, look, and listen**, or to count to five, may help delay their reactions; improved self-control usually diminishes their behavior problems.

Habit interruption is helpful when a youngster develops a nervous habit, such as biting his nails or twirling a lock of hair. The idea is to add minor inconvenient elements to the habit. This forces the child to be more aware of what he's doing, and also makes the practice more cumbersome—both of which discourage the behavior. For instance, a child who bites his nails might be instructed to clench his fists first for sixty seconds.

GROUP THERAPY

Sometimes children are treated in groups led by a qualified therapist. This form of therapy is especially beneficial when a youngster has problems with peer relationships. Participation in therapeutic groups can help him develop social skills and overcome timidity. Group treatment can be difficult to find and is more likely to be available in mental-health clinics than in a private practice.

Schools sometimes set up small groups, led by a guidance counselor or school psychologist, to deal with social issues. A group might be formed for youngsters who have difficulty cooperating or taking turns, in which they work on tasks or games designed to give them practice in these areas.

Support groups are available in many communities for children facing specific problems such as illness, divorce, death, or the alcoholism of a parent. These groups provide a safe way for youngsters to express their feelings among others who are going through similar experiences.

FAMILY THERAPY

A child's problems may stem, at least in part, from interactions within the family. In that case, treatment might be needed for the family as a whole or the parents as a couple.

I sometimes have sessions with an entire family as part of a treatment plan. But I am always aware that a child with emotional problems does not necessarily come from a dysfunctional family. I also work with couples on marital issues—provided they're willing to approach their problems cooperatively. But when I'm faced with a couple so hostile to each other that they are unable to cooperate, or with the rare family that is truly dysfunctional, I refer them to a marital or family therapist.

ADULT THERAPY

Sometimes the child is exposed to and excessively involved in the emotional problems of a father or mother. Simply making the parent aware of this is often sufficient to prompt change. Occasionally, though, a parent is so troubled, or his or her problems are so intertwined with those of the child, that improvements are not possible until the adult enters treatment.

PARENT GUIDANCE

Parent counselors and educators teach parents how to be more effective; they do not attempt to change personality at a deeper level. Education and counseling overlap, but educators usually lead groups and provide general instruction about child rearing, while counselors work with individual parents.

Parent guidance is a major part of my work, and I believe it should be a component in virtually all professional treatment of children. The younger the child, the more important it is to help his parents improve their understanding and management of him. However, I am cautious about applying standard solutions to specific families. A temperament-based approach, which is focused on the individual child, is an excellent model that is being used by a growing number of professionals.

Parent guidance was the key in my treatment of Owen, age three. His mom and dad were afraid that something was seriously wrong with their son: He frequently hit other children; he was selfish and wanted his own way all the time. They told me that he seemed to be hiding a lot of anger.

In my examination of Owen, I found no psychiatric problems. However, his parents were caught up in a vicious circle of ineffective action. Owen was an excitable boy, easily overstimulated, and also stubborn and persistent. Typically, they would overreact to his mis-behavior, then guiltily overindulge him afterward.

Rather than working directly with Owen, I met with his mother and father. I explained that most of his aggressive behavior was not cruel or angry or selfish, but impulsive; we developed a plan for early intervention. Negative persistence was the reason for his stubbornness; to deal with it, I suggested they take a stand early and bring discussions to an end. These and other measures—all carried out by the parents—sufficed to improve his behavior to their satisfaction.

MEDICATION

Properly prescribed and adequately monitored, medication is increasingly recognized as an effective form of treatment for children. Drugs can have positive effects on emotions and behavior, and thereby support other therapeutic changes in the youngster's life.

Many parents have reservations about using drugs to treat children's emotional problems. One reason for their concern is that medications can have troublesome side effects. These may be physical (e.g., dry mouth, constipation, headache); cognitive (e.g., dullness, difficulty concentrating); behavioral (e.g., withdrawal, fatigue); or emotional (e.g., angry outbursts, crying). Much less commonly, a child has an atypical reaction that is more serious. It's important to inform the prescribing physician if your child is taking medication and experiences any unusual physical, behavioral, or emotional change. Often the specific drug or the dose can be adjusted to reduce or eliminate side effects.

Medication must be prescribed by a physician, such as a child psychiatrist, pediatrician, family doctor, pediatric neurologist, or a psychopharmacologist—a psychiatrist who specializes in treatments involving medication. If the child is in therapy with a non–M.D., a medical doctor will be needed to manage the medication component of treatment; the therapist usually can help arrange this.

Unfortunately, some doctors who prescribe medication for emotional symptoms view drugs as the definitive treatment for a chronic illness. I would be concerned if a physician simply renewed the prescription every few months. Treatment should always include other measures and ongoing assessment.

When I use medication, I think of it not as the cure, but as part of a broader treatment plan. I prescribe the smallest effective dose, and once the situation is stable, I check to see how the child fares off the drug.

I find medication useful under the following circumstances:

- *To buy time in a crisis.* Medication can produce rapid, dramatic improvements that allow beleaguered adults to put long-term solutions into place. I used it that way with Billy, a seven-year-old with long-standing sleep problems: He refused to go to bed alone, and he woke up frequently in the middle of the night demanding attention.

During our first session, I helped his parents identify the family practices that contributed to these problems; we worked out several promising solutions, including simple rules and a twenty-minute bedtime routine. But at our second meeting, Billy's parents confessed that they had not been able to implement these changes consistently: They were simply too exhausted. Sedating Billy at night until his parents could catch up on their sleep helped them begin their new approaches.

▪ *For specific symptoms or disorders.* Certain symptoms respond well to medication, including bedwetting, phobias, compulsive behavior, and separation anxiety. I use drugs for these problems when other measures, such as behavioral techniques, are only partly effective.

The more seriously troubled the child, the more likely I am to prescribe medication. If the problems are extensive enough to justify a clinical diagnosis (for example, attention-deficit/hyperactivity disorder, obsessive-compulsive disorder, or an affective disorder such as major depression), drugs generally are an important part of treatment.

▪ *Temporary help.* Sometimes a child needs short-term assistance. Improved management at home and school had allowed Margot, a hyperactive eight-year-old, to stop taking Ritalin. But her parents called me in mid-November to ask if they could use it over Thanksgiving weekend: They were going to a family reunion, which had previously overstimulated Margot, and didn't think their usual management methods would work adequately away from home. Three days on Ritalin enabled Margot to get through the event successfully.

It's important to recruit the child as a collaborator when medication is used. The parent or the doctor should explain the purpose of the drug. For example, a parent might tell a seven-year-old boy who is about to receive Ritalin: "You're getting into a lot of trouble at school because it's really hard for you to control yourself when it's busy and noisy. That's not your fault. This medicine will help you feel calmer."

Children should be instructed to bring any side effects to their parents' attention. They also should be encouraged to express their feelings about taking medication. Sometimes youngsters are embarrassed about having to visit the school nurse's office for their daily dose. If this is an issue, ask the doctor if a long-acting form of the drug is available, so it need not be taken during the school day.

ENDING THERAPY

Ideally, your child's treatment will end when the goals of therapy have been met. But sometimes there's little or no progress, and it's not clear if therapy should continue. In either case, it's best to explore the situation fully with the therapist.

WHEN THERAPY DOESN'T SEEM TO BE WORKING

Suppose your child isn't improving, or he resists going to therapy sessions. He might say, "I have better things to do with my time" or "This is boring." Or problems may develop between you and the therapist.

Don't terminate treatment impulsively. When a child suddenly asks to stop seeing a therapist, he may unconsciously be avoiding painful but necessary parts of the process. But if a basically open and trusting youngster resists going to the therapist, his views should be given more weight.

A child who is very guarded, defensive, or oppositional may take a long time to develop a relationship with a therapist, and therefore a long time to show benefits from treatment. Also be aware that improvement is not always linear. More often the course of treatment will be uneven, and may even include periods where things temporarily get worse.

Slow progress and regression are disappointing. The blaming and defensiveness that can surface vis-à-vis a teacher when there are problems in school also can enter the relationship between parent and therapist. Problems between the two of you might also reflect a personality clash or a significant difference of values. Consider carefully if the difficulties reflect your personal issues, or if the therapist really isn't right for your family.

Try to discuss your concerns with the therapist in a neutral, collaborative way; he should be open to such a discussion. Ask questions. If the therapist has advised you to make certain changes and they haven't worked, say so and ask, "Can you suggest anything else?" Review the goals of treatment; perhaps information acquired since the initial evaluation has rendered his original impressions obsolete.

If you have tried unsuccessfully to clarify your concerns and feel that your reaction doesn't reflect defensiveness and anxiety, trust your judgment. Consider getting a second opinion if you're not sure.

WHEN THE PROBLEMS HAVE BEEN RESOLVED

The question of ending therapy also arises when things are going well for your child. Unless a fixed termination date is part of the treatment plan, I suggest that you refrain from interfering with a winning combination too quickly.

There are different ways to approach termination. My usual practice is to end gradually, on an experimental basis. If the child has had weekly appointments, we make it once every two weeks and then once a month. Extra sessions can be scheduled if there is slippage between visits or if a new problem arises. I also suggest to most families that they return for periodic follow-ups, to review, reassess, and tune up solutions. The door is kept open, unless there is a strong therapeutic reason for closing it.

OTHER OPTIONS

Children with emotional problems also can be helped by resources outside the mental-health profession. Some of the possibilities mentioned on the following pages are more traditional than others. I advise parents to be open-minded, but to maintain their focus on the needs of their particular child.

THE CHILD'S DOCTOR

Your family doctor or the child's pediatrician can be a valuable resource for emotional and behavioral as well as physical problems. A humane, broadly trained, and accessible doctor, whose interest encompasses the whole child, can be very helpful and in some instances obviate the need for psychiatric treatment. Increasingly, pediatric and family practices offer mental-health services for children and their parents, including parenting classes and support groups; the staff may include a child psychologist, a social worker, or a nurse-practitioner trained to provide parent education.

Here are some ways your child's doctor can help with emotional problems:

- *Ruling out physical causes.* Many symptoms and illnesses in children—especially those partly related to stress, such as headaches, stomachaches, dizziness, ulcers, irritable bowel syndrome, and asthma—have both a physical and psychological component. While it's obviously important to identify a treatable physical cause, excessive investigations should be avoided.

If the initial checkup yields no physical problem and further testing is recommended, ask questions: Why is this being done? What are the odds of finding the problem that is being ruled out? What might happen if we wait? Is there anything simpler we could do first? I have seen youngsters with stomachaches clearly related to going to school who have been put through barium swallows, sigmoidoscopy, and even surgery. Certain neurological investigations are overdone for youngsters with learning problems or hyperactivity.

- *Parent guidance.* The doctor can explain normal development, give you general advice, and answer specific questions about particular problems. Request a longer appointment (which may cost more) if you wish to discuss behavioral questions.

- *Neutral authority.* If your child has a physical problem with emotional components, the doctor can help you explain the situation to him. Sometimes the physician, a neutral but strong authority figure, can defuse battles in medical areas. If you and your child are struggling about problems like diet, bowel habits, or medication, let the doctor talk to the child directly.

The special problems of children with handicaps and chronic illnesses are beyond the scope of this book. I find that these youngsters show a surprising absence of severe psychiatric disorder. Such children and their families may, however, benefit from specialized guidance dealing with both medical and emotional issues; behavioral approaches for reducing stress; and support groups.

ALTERNATIVE APPROACHES

I respect therapies that focus on wellness and health, rather than on illness. The mind and body clearly are interdependent, and factors outside the scope of conventional medical understanding affect how we feel and behave. Alternative approaches recognize this wider range of contributing ingredients. They address environmental conditions, nutrition, exercise, stress reduction, and spiritual dimensions such as the importance of tranquility and the concept of balance. In recent years, treatments that once were considered unorthodox, like meditation and yoga, have found their way into mainstream medicine, particularly for adults.

At the same time, there are practitioners who promise too much or suggest that one solution fits all. Parents who aren't getting the hoped-for results through conventional mental-health or medical approaches are vulnerable to such promises. If alternative approaches sound helpful and involve no danger, I encourage you to experiment with them. Like medication, these treatments should always be part of a comprehensive plan.

DIET AND ALLERGIES

There is growing evidence that diet and allergies to food and environmental pollutants can contribute to behavior disorders in certain children. When parents tell me they are investigating such a connection, I advise them to trust their instincts and pursue the link, even if their child's doctor is skeptical.

Be aware, however, that significant modifications in your child's environment or lifestyle may be required. If your child is placed on an elimination diet, try to avoid power struggles by involving her as a collaborator.

Parent Education and Support Groups

Parenting books or classes, and informal or organized parent groups can be a valuable source of information and assistance. These may be general, or focused on a specific area such as learning disabilities. Look to them for support, information on normal development, and useful child-rearing tips. However, none of these can replace your knowledge of your own child. Don't overload yourself with information to the point that you are creating more anxiety than is relieved.

Community Resources

A child's emotional well-being can be enhanced by participation in community activities. Many recreational programs support therapeutic goals by building self-confidence, promoting cooperation and independent functioning, and improving social skills.

A shy youngster with artistic talent might develop friendships in a museum art class. Hyperactive, impulsive children benefit from structured physical activities that teach discipline and self-control, such as karate, swimming, gymnastics, or track and field. An overly dependent child can learn to be more self-sufficient by attending a carefully chosen overnight camp.

■　　■　　■　　■

Professional treatment is only one part of a total approach to helping your child. The options described in this chapter are not substitutes for the improvements you can make to foster your child's well-being—but ways to complement these efforts.

A FEW FINAL WORDS

The most gratifying part of my work is seeing the transformations that result when parents apply the principles of adult leadership. Changes in their attitude and approach, often seemingly minor, initiate a positive cycle: The child's favorable response generates good feelings in the parents, which in turn creates further progress. Over time, this cumulative process profoundly alters the atmosphere in the family, and many mild-to-moderate problems melt away.

This book is based on one of the forms of treatment I use in my psychiatric practice: brief parent guidance. An initial evaluation is followed by one to five sessions with the parents. After this, the family often is ready to move forward on their own.

Even if the difficulties aren't fully resolved, improvements are readily apparent at our final meeting. Everyone seems happier and more relaxed. The parents are friendlier to each other and to the child; they look less burdened and more confident in their authority. And if I ask the youngster about the problems that originally brought him to my office, he often dismisses them with a comment like, "Oh, that happened a long time ago."

As we talk, it's clear that communication is improving, and that family members are taking steps toward collaborating on solutions. "We had a planned discussion, and it really worked," a mother may tell me with amazement. "He's actually trying!"

The parents now see their child more clearly: They recognize her limitations as well as her strengths, and truly appreciate her for who she is. With increased understanding, their benevolent parenting instincts surface. A dad who previously insisted, "She's just trying to get me angry," may say, "I wish she wouldn't do that, but I know she often can't stop herself—and I'm trying to help her."

Discipline has become more effective. Instead of reacting to misbehavior, parents are planning preventive measures. Little by little, a family structure is created that will guide the youngster to greater success.

A family that has made this kind of turn-around has come a long way. If you've reached a similar point from applying the information in this book, you have achieved a great deal.

In my practice, I often recommend that parents return for a "check-up" six months to a year after we work together. I suggest you do the same: Every few months, sit down as a family and reassess the situation. This will help you maintain the improvements for which you've worked so hard.

Don't be overly discouraged by minor setbacks. A little bit of backsliding doesn't mean failure; nor do occasional errors reverse an overall change for the better. The youngster may have bad days; you may overreact, then guiltily feel that you've lost it. Allow yourself, your spouse, and your child the humanity to make mistakes. If you once again apply the principles of improved communication, understanding, acceptance, and discipline, you'll soon get back on track.

Being a parent is one of the most challenging tasks a human being can face. In our hands lies the enormous responsibility of guiding our children to the threshold of adulthood. We want so much for them: that they realize their full potential and find a satisfying niche in life; that they know the joy of loving others and being loved in return; and above all, that they feel contentment with themselves.

Laying the foundation that makes this possible isn't easy; almost inevitably, problems occur along the way. Because our hearts are so strongly engaged, these difficulties are very painful. No matter what else we do, and regardless how much we achieve in other areas of our lives, it's impossible for us to feel truly successful or at peace if something is seriously wrong with our child.

Over and over, I have seen mothers and fathers reach deep inside themselves and find the resources to make positive changes. If you are able to do the same, you will experience a resurgence of happiness and pride, not only in your child but in yourself. And if I have contributed to your efforts in this regard, then my purpose in writing this book has been truly fulfilled.

INDEX

ABOUT THE AUTHORS

STANLEY TURECKI, M.D., is a psychiatrist, author, and lecturer. He is a diplomate of the American Board of Psychiatry and Neurology, certified in adult and child psychiatry, and Assistant Clinical Professor of Psychiatry at the Mount Sinai School of Medicine in New York City. He is also on the attending staff of Beth Israel Medical Center and Lenox Hill Hospital, and a member of several professional organizations. In 1983, he founded the Difficult Child Program at Beth Israel, and in 1985 the Difficult Child Center in Manhattan.

Since the publication of *The Difficult Child* in 1985 (revised edition, 1989), Dr. Turecki has become widely known for his expertise on children and families. His views have been featured in many professional and popular publications, including *The New York Times*, *People*, *Redbook*, *Parents*, *Ladies' Home Journal* and *Working Mother*. His many radio and television appearances include *Good Morning America*, *The Today Show*, *CBS This Morning*, *Oprah Winfrey*, and *20/20*.

While maintaining an active practice in New York City, Dr. Turecki frequently lectures to parents, teachers, pediatricians, nurses, and mental health professionals, speaks at professional association functions, and regularly participates in the T. Berry Brazelton National Seminar series.

SARAH WERNICK, PH.D., is a freelance writer based in Brookline, Massachusetts, who specializes in health and family issues. She is a contributing editor for *Working Mother*; her articles also have appeared in *Woman's Day*, *Parents*, *Redbook*, *The New York Times*, and other publications.